The Tow and I
From Chairlifts to Sand Traps

PEG KURLANDER

– DEDICATION –

This book is dedicated to my parents, Jim and Agnes McGeehin
and my siblings, Jack McGeehin and Claire Hekker. Family always came first in our home. As kids, all of us found jobs cutting
lawns, baby sitting and getting a "real" job as soon as we were old
enough to obtain working papers. Our first introduction to skiing
was taking a curtain rod, bending it, somehow strapping it to our
boots and sliding down Hendel Avenue in North Arlington.
I regret that none of my immediate family ever learned to ski
and enjoy the beauty of North West New Jersey with us. The
Depression precluded our being able to afford those wonderful
adventures. I also know how proud they would be today to read
about Jack and Peg's adventures in Sussex County.

– CONTENTS –

– ACKNOWLEDGEMENTS –

Thanks to all my friends for their encouragement while I was writing this book. Their enthusiasm for the project has been a strong motivating force.

Thanks to Jack's golfing buddies for their support of the Jack Kurlander Memorial Foundation and the Jack Kurlander Memorial Golf Tournament fund raisers. They enabled us to award scholarships to worthy graduating students to help them with college expenses. (To date, the Foundation has given a total of 61 scholarships.) Special thanks to Richard Brennan and John Carrico who handled the funds and record-keeping. And to Ron Roth for his efforts to get the tournament/scholarship program started. And thanks to Lee Brennan for putting up with the amount of time Richard devoted to the Foundation.

Many other friends helped to make this book a reality. Included in that list is Joe Riggs, who gave me the information on Swedeland Forge's efforts to make the Crystal Springs Golf Community a success.

Kudos go to Lura Mountford for editing and doing research for the book. Thanks go to Susan Egan, Linda Freeman, Ginny Campbell, Debbie Leavitt, Maureen McGeehin, Leith Brennan and Carole Huettig for proofreading the story for me, keeping my writing errors to a minimum. John Kurlander was a tremendous help keeping me from forgetting to hit "Save" after I finished writing a chapter and teaching me how to forward a file. His computer skills were so welcomed. I wonder how anyone wrote a book before the PC era.

Special thanks go to Art Walton, VP of Golf at Crystal Springs Resort, for detailing the chronology and history of the Golf Mecca. And thanks to Gene Mulvihill for filling me in on some of the behind-the-scenes, humorous episodes we experienced along the way.

Harry Hicks added a touch of humor with his stories of the beginning days at Great Gorge – along with his Bert and Harry rendition of the George Washington Birthday advertisement and the bus from the Port Authority.

Sharron Mueller did a fine job with the book design and placement of photos and overseeing the printing process for The Tow and I. All of this was completed in the middle of a move from Vernon, New Jersey to her new home in Durango, Colorado.

– INTRODUCTION –

This is the story of how one man, gifted with extraordinary vision and enthusiasm, could, in a period of forty years, forever remake the footprint of Sussex County, NJ. The story is remarkable on several counts. In 1960 Sussex County was predominantly rural farmland occupied by more cows than people.

At this writing in 2011 much of the county's farmland and its related agrarian industry have awakened from their rural slumbers to become a vacation destination, one predominantly recreational in outlook. Our little corner of Northwestern New Jersey now lures countless visitors to its winter sports and its summer golfing. Miraculously, much of its pastoral charm remains. All who have witnessed this remarkable evolution agree that credit as the catalyst and driving force that forged this change belongs to Jack Kurlander. His story is my story. The story tells how one man's dream became reality. Most importantly, looking back, the chance to help turn his dream into reality was a gift I would not exchange for any other I can imagine.

So why tell this particular story? Picture how interested or excited you would be to read about a man who manufactured plastic spoons. For that matter, who would want to read about a woman's experiences as the wife of a manufacturer of toasters, detergents, ball point pens or automatic ski waxers. Automatic ski waxers, you ask? Well that is just part of a story that does get told later in this book. Even more compelling, however, are the many challenges we met and overcame in our far from ordinary career paths from chairlifts to sand traps.

My first attempt to write this book was in 1993. This time around about all that remains of that initial effort is the book's title, *The Tow and I*. A subtitle has recently been added to the cover entitled *From Chairlifts to Sand Traps*.

With gratitude to Betty MacDonald and her 1945 epic *The Egg and I* we gained by her description of life on a remote farm in the State of Washington. *The Tow and I* strikes a similar resonating note about being transported to sleepy rural Sussex County and living for forty-plus years in the vortex of its evolution.

When we arrived on the scene in 1964 and settled in Vernon, we were regarded as "them there (pronounced 'thar') city folk". Our three young kids played after school and then went home for "dinner". Local folks went home for "suppa". When we first came to Vernon to live, we actually thought we had moved to McAfee. Turns out McAfee, pronounced Mac-A-Fee by some Scotsmen long before we Irish settled here, is actually only a post office designation of that section of the more inclusive Vernon.

Local lore tells us that as early as the 1940's, a rudimentary rope tow was set up and ran roughly 200 feet up the hill that is now the lowest section of current-day Mountain Creek. This revolving rope eliminated the need to hike or climb and was used to pull adventurous winter skiers to the top. Once the skier detached himself from the rope at the top of the small patch of snow, he risked life and limb by sliding down again on his long wooden skis.

Local folks (pronounced 'foke') knew the area and its labor-saving attraction only as "that thar ski tow." Hence the locals began by referring to our wonderful project as "down thar at the ski tow." No matter how hard we tried we could not convince the locals that we were not like the sophisticated skiers of pishy poshy Stratton Mountain in Vermont, although we rather thought we were. Nor could we educate them to the idea that our new endeavor should be referred to as a "ski area" or even hopefully as a "ski resort" rather than just another rope tow attraction. When I think back on this period of our earliest dreams and all that came after, I still marvel at the vision of the man I married in 1953. Characteristic of Jack was how he always managed to keep our plans and our setbacks in perspective. Often what sustained him was talking about how what we were trying to build might impact on what came next. Jack, ever the well-read historian, loved to speculate about time capsules which may be been opened some two centuries hence full of lift tickets, dimpled golf balls and area brochures. "Just imagine," he would often say, "archeologists puzzling over the bits and remains of my old six-foot-seven-inch Atomic Arcs. When tee-shaped towers and bits of welded steel attached to a wire that might be or might not be part of a chair surface from the dig, what will they think?"

Because he was a life-long optimist, however, his interpretation of our place in history was never more than a diverting what-if mind game. What truly sustained the dream were thoughts of building a place where others could learn what ski purists feel as they fly down a snow-filled mountainside. What sustained him most of all was in believing our place in downtown McAfee would be where new converts to the love of skiing could share his dream. Historians, archeologists, and other advanced human life forms may someday ponder the mysteries of our little Shangri-La tucked into the outer reaches of an east coast megalopolis. We are the lucky ones who know the details of how it all happened.

What follows is the story of how this recreational Shangri-La came to be and, once begun, how the path of its footprints twisted and turned until it became a premier recreational destination for the greater New York/New Jersey Metropolitan area.

The Kurlander Family – 50th Anniversary – Black Bear Golf Club

– CHAPTER 1 –

FAMILY HISTORY

Although not directly bearing on the resort industry in Sussex County, our family background is an important ingredient of this story and sheds some light on the drive and inspiration that motivated us.

John Leonard Kurlander, known ever after as Jack, was born on October 2, 1929 in Providence, Rhode Island and raised in Nutley, New Jersey. Not much is known about Jack's parents. What is known helps explain why his ability to think "out of the box" might be considered a genuine birthright. Jack's father, John Henry Kurlander, also known as Hans, was born in the 1880's in Rhode Island and was educated in the field of electrical engineering.

His mother, Martha Behrens, emigrated from Germany, presumably to the Providence area, in the early 1900's. Her name is on the wall at Ellis Island and her entry as an immigrant is recorded on the lists maintained there. After clearing the rigorous Ellis Island inspections, Martha found work as a nanny and soon met John in Providence.

After John and Martha married, the family moved to Nutley, New Jersey when John Henry took a job with Westinghouse. He worked there for many years as Westinghouse's leading electrical engineer. During the period of young Jack's formative years, from 1934-1949, his father developed and held patents for most of the products related to lighting that the company manufactured. John Henry's patents included those for fog lights, automobile sealed-beam headlights, and most of the electrical lighting components used in the burgeoning movie industry, including a 1,000 watt incandescent projection lamp to show home movies. Unlike today's world where each new creation in the venture capital-internet era is handsomely rewarded, corporate loyalty prevailed and there were no thoughts of "get rich quick." As a condition of his employment all of John Henry's patents were sold to Westinghouse for $1.00 each.

The intrinsic rewards were substantial, however, two of the most impressive patents he held proved vital to our success in World War II. Both of these important patents helped bring critical aid and reassurance for air force crews engaged in combat. The first was for a gun scope, the multi-lenticular collimating gun sight device and optical system. The scope permitted fighter pilots to see Japanese Kamikaze planes with the sun shining from directly behind them, normally a blind spot for the naked eye. Pilots using the scope gained an early detection advantage in spotting enemy planes coming at them in the direction of the sun's rays. Planes thus equipped with the Kurlander gun scope then had a chance to shoot first and talk later. Their survival rates improved greatly.

The second equally impressive patent was one granted to John Henry in 1942 for a light bulb, the size of a walnut, which could throw a beam of light over two hundred miles. The light quickly became standard equipment on the life rafts of all planes used during the later stages of the war. It enabled Air Force crews who had their planes shot down and been forced into life rafts to be located and rescued. Use of this long-range beam of light proved invaluable to our rescue planes, most especially those searching the vast Pacific waters.

Over the years, Jack's father John Henry also came to be highly regarded for his work in projection optics. This led to his election as Secretary of the Motion Picture Engineers Society. As part of his duties as the society secretary, he often met and worked with Thomas Edison at both his West Orange and Menlo Park Laboratories. Equally challenging were the days he was called to consult with Albert Einstein in Princeton.

Meanwhile, Martha was what is now known as a stay-at-home mom. There she raised two active and lively boys, Jack, and, senior by two years, older brother Bob. In answer to the challenge of their perpetual motion activities, she was often heard to state: "Let's hope for the best." Looking back on her nearly a century later, one can still sing her praises as a great mother and mother-in-law.

Growing up, Jack was always innovative, trying to reinvent the wheel, perhaps trying to emulate his inventor father. Throughout high school his main focus was on sports. He competed successfully in track and was a fine tennis player. By his senior year at Nutley High School his athletic skills began to attract attention. In the spring of 1949 he won the individual state singles tennis championship and was recognized as the top high school tennis

player in New Jersey. Outside of school Jack was active in Boy Scouts and various Boys Club activities. Through them, he spent many weekends camping in the Adirondacks and enjoying other outdoor adventures such as climbing Mt. Marcy. More important to the story, this is where he first learned to ski and was captured by its powerful attraction.

Not surprising with such an inventive heritage and an encouraging mother, young Jack grew up energetic and "thinking big." The family sought help on how best to channel this budding talent. When Jack was a senior at Nutley High School, his father drove him to Stevens Institute for a career assessment and evaluation. Fortuitously, after several hours of testing, the administering professor emerged to tell his parents that Jack should build a ski area or at least explore career opportunities in that field.

Jack, Glenn, Big Ronnie, Walter, Fred & friends

That settled and tucked securely in the back recesses of his mind, our young entrepreneur set out to gain needed experience. Jack first tried a year of college. Too impatient for the sedentary classroom experience, next he answered the draft board's call for army service. Jack spent his two-year stint during the Korean War at Fort Devens, the Ayer, Massachusetts Training Center and School for Army Security and Traffic Analysts. His job there was to serve as recreation instructor teaching skiing and tennis to trainees stationed on the base. The army also capitalized on his athletic ability by selecting him to represent the base in inter-service tennis competitions. He began his military career as a lowly private, rose in the ranks to sergeant, and just as quickly when chaffing under some of the more strict military regulations regarding off-limits behavior, found himself honorably discharged with a private first-class ranking. No specifics are known here except to say Jack felt that if a Jeep sat idle on the base and he needed a ride into town it seemed okay to "borrow" it for the evening.

Lean-to on Mount Marcie, Adirondack's – Cornie Lorenzen & Jack at 17

Once his initial tour of duty was over, Jack moved on to the working world. To earn money for college expenses he tried selling Kirby vacuum cleaners and quickly proved himself to be a natural salesman. (It's interesting to note that Gene Mulvihill also learned his salesmanship skills selling Kirby Vacuum Cleaners. Makes one wonder if that was an omen or a harbinger of things to come in their lives.) Women who were already happy with a working vacuum cleaner of a lesser brand found themselves charmed by the young man with the exuberant enthusiasm and captivating claims. Their old machines worked perfectly well, but they bought into the dream of having a shiny new look. This same persuasive confidence he now used to land a sales job in Columbus, Ohio. The job went well, but he missed New Jersey and happily took another job closer to home.

On the other hand, my early experiences took a somewhat different direction. My parents, Agnes and Jim McGeehin, were hard-working and loving. Jim was often called Big Jim, a nickname that referenced his rather diminutive height, he being all of five feet three inches tall. Jim was a tool and die maker by trade and was employed over the years by several different manufacturing companies in New Jersey. To supplement what he earned, Agnes worked as a secretary for a New Jersey branch of the DuPont Chemical Company. She was so highly regarded there that when several of the enterprising young engineers left to form their own spin-off, Chemplast Corporation, they insisted she become the office manager of their new operation. The company thrives to this day and Agnes McGeehin continues to be a part of its legend. One of its early corporate struggles involved creating paid holidays. Agnes, a devout Roman Catholic, insisted on adding Good Friday to the list. She wielded such clout that not only was it selected to be a paid holiday for employees of the company. It became known as Agnes' Day Off rather than its religious equivalent.

My parents lived and raised their family in several New Jersey locations. I started life in Orange, New Jersey on August 19, 1932. Soon afterward the family moved to Scotch Plains. My brother Jack, sister Claire and I grew up with modest means during the difficult Depression era of the 1930's. This meant that the family often struggled through some difficult days. For our family, living below our means were the operative words.

For example, bills were paid when there was sufficient money to do so. The kids of the family were taught to "duck down" and hide when the milkman came to collect money on certain difficult Saturdays. Usually, by the next, week the problem was solved and no duck-down commands were issued. I am told that one Saturday I met the milkman and started chatting with him. I arrived at a point when I spoke to him in the gravest of tones, saying to him, "My mommy does not want to answer the door. We were ducking down and we had to be very quiet because we had no money." Agnes arrived on the scene and, with great dignity and humor, stated: "She is such a chatter box. Don't listen to all she has to say." Smiling excuses, she then offered a portion of the small sum due to the milkman. I suspect he understood the situation.

The onset of World War II and the years that followed brought improved job prospects for the McGeehin family. Jim's tool and die expertise was in demand, and DuPont hired Agnes for her ability to organize and run an office efficiently. The family moved once more, settling happily in their permanent North Arlington home.

In contrast to Jack's early sporting life, my talents moved in a musical direction. After-school hours were spent learning to play piano and eventually organ at the Queen of Peace Church in North Arlington. The church and the high school were run in the same building. The nuns were very strict and demanded excellence from anyone enrolled at this high school. Most of my classmates worked after school to help pay for their education and many were hired as file clerks at the Prudential Insurance Company in Newark. When the dismissal bell rang each day we ran to the corner, caught the 102 bus which carried us to the very tall building in time to catch an elevator up to the 8th floor. We dashed to our designated file locations where we worked until 6:00 pm, finding and moving files to the accounting department where weekly 25¢ premiums were recorded on file cards. These were in the days when the insurance salesman walked to the insured's home every Saturday, collected the 25¢ premium and took it to the big building in Newark. All of us clerks loved our jobs and traveled together on public buses. Every night I caught a bus in Newark and went to a church in Kearny where I was studying organ with a renowned Italian organist, Professor Varche. It was very exciting playing the massive organ at St. Stephen's Church where I went to practice five nights a week. During the winter months it was pretty spooky climbing to the choir loft after dark with only small flickering votive lights to guide the way. I practiced the music of Bach, Debussy and Beethoven for an hour, and then left the church to catch another bus to North Arlington. I then walked two miles to home. There were still some piano lessons to practice and often homework assignments followed. Most nights I went to bed around midnight and rose the next morning at 6:00 am. I am sure the child labor officials today would never allow this kind of a schedule for a student. My classmates and I loved all of it. I guess I was a workaholic.

My parents, who were wonderful roll models, were supportive of all the endeavors of my teen years. I often wonder how they were able to afford enough money to support the private school and private music opportunities. My paycheck from Prudential helped a little. All of us clerks were paid one dollar an hour and worked 15 hours a week. In the summer we worked full time and were paid $30 a week plus a free lunch at the cafeteria. My big splurge each week took place every Friday, which was pay day. We always cashed our checks and ran to purchase some delicious chocolate delicacies at Fanny Farmer Candy Shop at the corner of Broad and Market Streets. Some weeks I decided to purchase a beautiful chocolate éclair at one of Newark's fine bakeries.

My years at The Pru ended at graduation from high school in 1950. I don't know exactly what year computers took over our jobs. Today when I am working on my wonderful PC I think back to my years as a file clerk. I realize that computers have done wonderful things for the world. But I often think of the millions of file clerks, telephone operators and people whose jobs were lost and never replaced. How fortunate I was to be able to go to school, work at a wonderful after school job, earn money for college, study music and attend a fine high school. I was blessed to have the support of my family throughout my life.

My introduction to skiing was purely social and little has changed since the sport was popularized. I had heard ski slopes were one of the best places to meet boys and enjoy a bit of fun. A few friends and I left school one week-end and headed to the New York Port Authority to take a bus to Belleayre, a popular ski resort area in the Catskills. We were too naïve to inquire if the area had any snow or whether snow conditions were important. We figured that if people were going to a ski area, of course the area would have snow. That first night we checked into an old hotel in the town of Pine Hill and hurried off to a local square dance being held at the local Grange, all the while scarcely noticing that not a single flake of snow covered the ground nearby. Fortuitously, we awakened that next morning to a world turned white. We headed up to the slopes to take a lesson from Jim Anders of the Belleayre Ski School. By day's end we had learned to do a respectable snow plow turn and fancied ourselves skiers! It's interesting to note that the skis I used on my first ski trip were carved out of maple and had no metal edges. I dressed in a beautiful grey hand-knit woolen Tyrolean-style sweater. My parents had purchased these two items which they gave me for Christmas that year. Both items were purchased at Macy's Department Store.

After that weekend my friends and I checked around and heard about the Twin Hickory Ski Club, which met on Wednesday nights a VFW in nearby Nutley. Its reputation as one of the oldest and best in the state assured us that it might have a roster of eligible and appealing college-age skiers interested in the club's active social calendar. At our first meeting my eyes quickly turned to the club's energetic leader who brimmed with plans for future ski trips. In turn, I caught the eye of that same club president who interrupted his summarizing of planned outings to inquire about the pretty new face that caught his attention. Another member told him the "new girl" played the piano. Thinking fast, Jack, as Club President, made an executive decision and announced that the club was starting a band and that, after the regular meeting adjourned, there would be a special meeting in the bar. He went on to add that the band had particular need for a back-up pianist.

Reflecting on this oft-repeated story, what I remember most was the electric effect of meeting such a charismatic person. Physically he was not overpowering, being of medium height and a compact athletic build. His electric blue eyes, ready smile, and quick, rapid movements, however, made him hard to overlook. Riveting seems a better choice of words, perhaps. Riveted I was, then, and in all the many days that followed.

Nature and proximity soon took care of the rest. Within a few short months the romance had progressed and I felt propelled forward, caught up in a whirlwind courtship that ended in a July 23 wedding in 1954.

Thus began our rock-solid marriage and tumultuous life of riotous ups and downs that lasted for nearly 52 years. Our marriage of complementary strengths ended only when Jack's exuberant enthusiasm imploded in the midst of yet another visionary plan to transform one more unique recreational area. He died as he lived, talking enthusiastically while driving quickly, enthralled with his vision of the Connecticut landscape he had just discovered and envisioning how each piece of the terrain would soon meld golf course and comfortable living to become even greater than the last such project he had willed into life back in Sussex County, New Jersey.

– CHAPTER 2 –

EARLY ADVENTURES
FROM PACKANACK TO VERMONT

Married life for us began in rather typical fashion. Jack was happy working as a salesman selling lumber to North Jersey lumberyards, and I settled into the life of young housewife. Following our July wedding and brief honeymoon, we moved into a two-family apartment in Belleville, New Jersey. Not surprisingly, children arrived in rapid succession. John was born in June of 1956, followed by Jamie in November, 1957.

With another child on the way and the Belleville apartment growing smaller by the day, it was time for a move. Our little family found a wonderful Cape Cod "starter" house a block from the beach in the Packanack Lake section of Wayne, New Jersey. We moved in late 1958 and in time to welcome Judy, our third and final child, into the world in March of 1959.

The move was a good one on several counts. Jack was starting a new job as a salesman for Pacific Mutual Door Company, a company that sold windows and doors. Packanack Lake would be closer to most of his customers. The little lake community also proved to be a wonderful location for making life-long friends and for enjoying the outdoor sporting life Jack loved so well. Even though he was now a successful salesman, married with three children, he still had a restless itch to start or invent something that would let him work for himself and run his own show. He also had not given up his passion for skiing.

As a salesman with rather flexible hours, Jack often arranged his schedule so as to get in a few days of skiing at some of the New York ski areas or at nearby Craigmeur, the first ski area ever built in the northwest section of New Jersey. The skiing was supposed to be just for fun, but the business possibilities of combining this kind of recreation along with the fun continued to nag him.

At this time in the late 1950's, skis were still made of pine or hickory. Ski manufacturers were experimenting with screwing metal edge strips to the outside edges of the ski to give it more grip and tracking potential. Snow sticking to ski bottoms, however, continued to spoil many a downhill run. Skiers had to wax their skis by hand to make them slide faster, a time-consuming process and one that needed to be repeated, often after every trip down the mountain. Jack sensed that an "Automatic Ski Waxing Machine" was the perfect solution to the problem.

Unlike our first attempt to get rich quick, this time Jack was sure his latest enterprise would be a winner. Our earlier venture occurred shortly after we started married life in Belleville, New Jersey. Jack had thought we would make a fortune selling the long-lasting nylon tennis nets we so lovingly put together in the Nutley basement of Lorenzen's Bakery. I was seven months along in my first pregnancy but accompanied Jack every night to Nutley to sit at an over-sized commercial sewing machine and carefully stich the two or three pieces of netting and edging required to make a complete tennis net.

One night we were working in the basement and someone started sweeping the floor upstairs precipitating a powder storm leaking flour into the basement where the seamstress and the inventor were working on the new nets. The scene was reminiscent of a Lucille Ball Show episode where Lucy and Ethel are shown working in the chocolate factory trying to keep pace with the chocolates that were coming down the assembly line to their location. We tried to keep pace with the flour coming through the floor as we shook it out of our hair. It was a hopeless task. We returned home and quickly headed to a hot shower. Unfortunately, demand for new nets was limited and their labor-intensive, hand-tied knotting assembly process soon tried the limited patience of this most energetic of men.

Now a ski waxer, he reasoned, unlike a tennis net, could be monetized daily, and the supply of ready ski areas where a waxer could be installed was growing each year.

The design Jack envisioned was simple. As the skier got in line for a lift ride up the mountain, he would roll over wax-covered rollers that would rewax his skis. Next Jack joined forces with his friend, Harold Aulthen who had been a classmate at Nutley High School. Harold had skills in metals design work. The two of them built a prototype. As I recall, some of the work was done at the home of John and Ann Fitzgerald, friends from Twin Hickory Ski Club days. The Fitzgeralds lived in the Pines Lake section of Wayne, very near to our Packanack Lake house. Their basement offered room to experiment with various models of the ski waxer. After several months of trial and error, they had a workable machine. The final machine, complete with a coin-collection box, consisted of a large wooden frame that housed a series of wax-coated rollers. The rollers applied ski wax to the ski bottoms of any skier who inserted his coin and paid to walk with his skis on through the bare-framed housing. On July 24, 1962 Jack was awarded Patent #3,045,639 for his Automatic Ski Waxing Machine, the skier's dream of convenience.

Automatic Ski Waxing Machine

Next Jack came up with a business plan to have these machines manufactured and then installed at ski areas throughout the northeast. He hoped that his idea of a coin-vending add-on made the plan economically feasible. Typically, he was confident this innovation would soon become a necessary part of every skier's day – or so we thought. For better or for worse, we jumped right in. Jack, ever the optimistic salesman, was elected as the one to sell his new machine to as many ski area managers as he could reach. This meant a move to Vermont was required if we were to launch this new venture properly. This in turn meant uprooting the family and moving with the three young kids in tow to spend the winter of 1959-1960 in the granite state.

Housing was one of the first obstacles we overcame. Happily, Lee and Mary Morton appeared on the scene, anxious to rent a house while they looked for a more permanent home. Amazingly, after spending that first winter in Packanack, the Mortons bought a home there and have continued to be very good friends of ours ever since.

With the Packanack rental settled in favor of the Mortons, we packed our things into our old black and white Chevy station wagon and headed off to Vermont. The trip up was carefree and upbeat.

In the 1960's no one used car seats for their children. John and Jamie wrestled around on the back seat. Judy, then seven months old, was transported in an old rickety car bed which rocked and swayed all the way. Throughout the long six-hour drive, she was happy and content. Her siblings would take brief time outs from their tumbling to give her hugs and keep her cheered. Once in Vermont we found an old farm house on Route 7 on a hill just north of Manchester for rent. We moved in that night and set about to make our fortune.

We were excited about our move and too naïve to see the potential pitfalls we would encounter. The kids were young, there were no neighbors and the winter was both snowy and cold. None of our kids were of age to attend school and staying at home with them was not very glamorous.

Lessons learned from college days suggested marshalling resources at hand and employing diversionary activities might help stave off cabin fever. One of this writer's favorite memories of that long winter was one such effort. Throughout those long winter days while Jack was out tending his machines and socializing with the area operators, the stay-at-homes needed their own diversion. I hit on the idea of teaching the kids to make maple syrup. How hard could that be? The family learned quickly how difficult it is to find maple trees in the winter when there is no foliage on the trees – not that we could have identified a leafy maple tree even in summer! Undeterred, off we went with hammers and pots and other equipment determined to "collect our syrup."

The next problem was that even after we identified and tapped the proper tree, the tapped sap running from the tree only looked like yucky water, not the finished syrup we expected. We learned we had to boil the yucky water if we were to have any rewards for our efforts. This proved not an easy task since it involved our collecting some rather large soup pots, dumping the liquid into them and then boiling the yucky water for an inordinate amount of time. This we attempted on a 40 year-old electric stove which had only two burners still functioning.

After two days of boiling we were able to render about a cup of "syrup" from our first batch of tapped liquid. We tasted it. It needed some tweaking but we managed a passable sauce for our waiting pancakes. So much for that adventure. Purchasing a bottle of maple syrup at Shop Rite today still brings back memories of those Vermont days. A nice bottle of *Made in Vermont* maple syrup today costs less than $20. In retrospect, that sounds like a real bargain.

Another favorite memory from that Vermont winter involves the local Vermont telephone company. We shared our party line with three other families and became quite familiar with the local operator and the various talkers who happened to share our not very private conversations. Listening in was one of the more social parts of our day. We also always had the telephone number of the nearest fire station close at hand and prayed that someone would be there to take our midnight call if our fireplace sparked. Fortunately, that was one call we never had to make.

Meanwhile, Jack took off each day to visit his ski area operators and sell these pioneers in the business of ski area management a new way to speed up downhill ski time. Soon machines were installed at Bromley, Sugarbush, Mount Snow and Killington. All of our waxers were close enough to allow Jack frequent visits to these facilities to check on progress and encourage their use.

It took awhile for skiers to get the hang of using the waxing device. Jack's solution was to spend extra time at each area encouraging people to try this new way to have skis waxed. No matter how unforgiving the outdoor conditions, he enthusiastically walked up and down lift lines assuring every waiting skier that using the waxer would give them more time to enjoy his favorite sport.

At the end of each visit to a ski area the coins that had been collected were emptied from the waxer's collection box and divvied up with the owner or manager, "one-for-you and one-for-me-style." We spent most nights after the kids had gone to bed at the kitchen table wrapping the coins Jack had collected that day. The take was marginally lucrative. Thankfully, for the stockholders awaiting word back in New Jersey of new-found riches, no machines were ever broken open at night by vandals looking for ready cash.

When up that way, Jack's favorite place for the nightly coin exchange became the Wobbly Barn at the base of Killington Mountain. The barn can still be found on the access road to the mountain and remains in business as a local hangout for suds and buds. Jack often stopped by for chili and a burger and a chance to swap stories with Pres Smith. Pres had built and operated Killington and reveled in its growing success. Pres and his family* lived at the mountain and his stories of ski area living hit a responsive chord with Jack.

---

* Years later in the late 1970's Leslie Smith, daughter of Pres and Sue, competed with Jamie when they were both on the US Ski Team. In retrospect it would have been cheaper to help a daughter along to ski fame by sending her to a ski academy and paying the requisite tuition. But back then we were "Dreaming the Impossible Dream" of making it on our own. Old diary entries of Jack's reveal that Pres Smith later visited him at Hidden Valley during its early planning days and walked the trails with him. Pres was also there to check out our "state of the art" snowmaking, which today we would translate as used junk from Snow Bowl.

– CHAPTER 3 –

BACK TO REALITY

My parents developed major health issues in the winter of 1959-1960. They needed our attention. Our young kids also needed better schooling and some playmates their own age. Prudence dictated that it was time to head back to Jersey to be closer to family and the conveniences of suburban living. Income from the ski waxing business barely covered expenses. Plastic-bottomed skis began to be seen on ski slopes everywhere. New skis annually began to feature P-Tex bottoms making waxing a thing of the past. We faced up to the facts. Our Vermont adventure was over. We never looked back except to wonder occasionally where in Vermont the remains of our ski waxers were buried.

We returned to our Packanack Lake house at winter's end in 1960, and Jack went back to his job selling millwork. To make ends meet Jack also started working three nights a week at Frank Daley's Meadowbrook Dinner Theatre in Cedar Grove. His job there was to take photos of the customers, rush to the darkroom to develop and print the photos, and then hurry back to sell them to the customer. In between photographs, he cleared tables as people finished eating their dinners. His third job was selling furniture at a store in Wayne.

Another man might have minded extra burdens, but not Jack. He never complained. He left in the mornings, whistling, and was whistling when he arrived home in the evening. To everyone else, it sure seemed as though he was wearing rose-colored glasses every day. We, however, loved the funny stories of his busy days. He laughed and enjoyed the retelling as much as we, even when the joke was on him. On the rare nights he was not working, he met occasionally with "the guys" and enjoyed swapping stories, the best of which he brought home to retell to us for yet another happy laugh. One such source of new stories came from meetings he attended as a member of the

Concatenated Order of Hoo Hoo. This rather social group of men employed in the lumber industry met monthly under the guise of talking business to make connections and hear the latest industry scuttlebutt.

Jack's hectic schedule earned us enough money to allow me to be a stay-at-home mom with our three kids. How fortunate I was to have the opportunity to enjoy a luxury that few families can afford today. Even though Jack's main job was outside the home and mine was in it, when it came to the challenges of parenthood, we both worked together. Whenever possible, Jack was home for dinner, and I was happy to have the extra assistance through dinner, baths, pajama time and the kid's Book of the Night Club.

Although the house was small and all three kids slept in cribs crowded into one room, we tried hard to turn little discomforts into better times. When the basement flooded after a hard rain, which it often did, that became a game of paddling a little canoe around the washing machine area.

Living only one block from the beach meant summers were great fun. Early on, the kids learned to swim. From our earliest Packanack days with the beach serving as a people magnet, each of us quickly made good and long-standing friendships. The membership in our social group was loose. One need only be a parent of one of the children's newly acquired beach friends to be considered part of what was affectionately named the Play Pen Pals.

Play Pen Pals moms often were able to negotiate a break in the daily routine by swapping baby-sitting duties with another pal and his or her mom. For me, this opened up a chance to earn a little money as a substitute teacher in some of the Wayne schools.

Mary Morton, our friend who had lived in our home while we were in Vermont, also welcomed the chance to teach. The families matched up well when it came to exchanging baby-sitting duties. Mary especially loved to work with special education students and, as such, was a very popular sub. Mary's husband Lee had been called up for active duty in the Air National Guard and was assigned to France for air lift operations during the 1961 Berlin Wall crisis. Thanks to a few banked extra days of swapped child care, when the time came, she was able to make the trip to France for a few days' leave with Lee. Her kids happily piled into our house and everyone enjoyed the whole experience.

The person in charge of calling subs to work knew our skills and scheduled us accordingly. Children in Mary's special education classes were applauded if they learned to tie their shoes after three months of trying. On the other hand, I preferred handling kindergarten and the early grades where learning focused more on the standardized reading and math skills. Happily, our co-operative scheduler quickly mastered who best fit where.

My substitute teaching brought other kinds of challenges. One day I was subbing in a fourth grade classroom. A boy named Markie was very disruptive in class and refused to stay at his desk as instructed. I tried talking gently with him to convince him to sit and get his assignments done. Foolishly, I turned my back on him to help another child and saw the culprit running to the front of the room and making a dash for a window half open for ventilation. Markie bolted out the window and ran around an open field. I rushed to the emergency phone and pleaded with Mr. B., the principal, to send support. Mr. B. arrived on the scene and managed to tackle little Markie and get him back into his seat. I listened to Mr. B. trying the "Now Mark, why did you do this?" routine. Markie's unbowed reply of "Duhh, I just felt like getting some exercise", seemed to satisfy them both. I am not sure who learned what that day!

As a bit of follow-up to this story, I had gone to college with Mr. B. and felt a little betrayed by his idea of discipline. I sometimes wonder where Mark and Mr. B. are today. I know I never again agreed to return to that school when asked to sub there.

Our Packanack backyard had a nice incline. In the winter we made it into a little ski slope. An old clothes line became the "rope tow" used to get back up the slope. Just about then, Jack also started teaching skiing on weekends at the Snow Bowl Ski Area in Jefferson, New Jersey. Soon the whole family went skiing at Snow Bowl as often as we could get away. More and more often, our favorite family outing any free weekend day or even the occasional evening was to head to the ski slopes.

With little money to buy good equipment for the children, Jack improvised. He took some old wooden skis, cut them down to about two feet in length, and fashioned some kind of binding. We found some sturdy rubber Mickey Mouse boots that somehow he was able to fasten onto the skis. Rudimentary at best, but the kids adapted to this makeshift equipment. They quickly learned to be pretty skillful "snowplowers."

By now we were settled into a fun and "normal" life of family, friends and kids' activities. When we outgrew the little Packanack Lake Cape Cod house, we moved to a nearby ranch house just outside the lake area. From there we moved a few miles farther away to a home we built in the Lake Valhalla section of nearby Montville. Nothing had really changed much except our home was larger. We continued to enjoy our many friends and the weekends and occasional evenings we spent skiing at Snow Bowl. All this while, however, the dream to build his own ski area continued to gnaw at Jack. His job as an outside salesman required plenty of driving around southern New York, northern New Jersey, and eastern Pennsylvania. As the ensuing years attest, unknowingly this proved to be extremely important background research information. Little did he quite realize, these random paths afforded him the chance for an in-depth look at the topography of most of our surrounding regions. As we shall see, when the time was right, his research led him to Vernon's Hamburg Mountain. But that is a subject for the next chapter!

– CHAPTER 4 –

WE MEET THE MOUNTAIN

One day, in the spring of 1963, Jack came home from his salesman's job and announced that he had put a deposit on a mountain property in McAfee, New Jersey. We had only recently moved from Wayne to the house we built in the Lake Valhalla section of Montville to be closer to Jack's expanding territory. "McAfee", we asked, "where in the world is that?" What we soon learned is that they have a funny way of naming towns in New Jersey. Townships are often broken into sections, with each section named after their local post office. Hence, Vernon Township had sections labeled McAfee, Sussex, Vernon and Highland Lakes. Vernon Township was the recorded name of the property. Jack's mountain was in the McAfee section of the Township. What we soon also learned was that McAfee was worlds away from the kind of suburban existence we had grown accustomed to living in since our return from Vermont.

Naturally, Jack, bubbling with his usual enthusiasm, could hardly wait to have the family see this new treasure in his life. At the time Jack put down his deposit on the old Frederick's Farm in McAfee, Sussex County offered very little winter recreation for its residents. We heard that sometime in the early 1940's there had once been a little rope tow running roughly 200 feet up the mountain behind the Frederick's barn. It had long since disappeared. A few other rope tows driven by make-shift auto engines had been tested on various other county farms that had steep sloping hills as a part of their properties. Each of these early tows had enjoyed only limited runs over the years. The only existing alpine-type areas in the early 1960s that might qualify as true "ski areas" were the well-established learn-to-ski destination Craigmeur Ski Area in Newfoundland and Snow Bowl, which operated in Jefferson Township. No one had yet thought of the Hamburg Mountain site in the McAfee section of Vernon Township as a destination that would attract serious skiers coming from beyond the county borders.

Early the next day we piled John, Judy, and Jamie into our old station wagon for our first visit to what was to become Great Gorge. We parked the car beside the little farm house that fronted on the old country road version of Route 94 and started inspecting. We took in the large, rather dilapidated barn, that also fronted on the road and noticed several other small outbuildings. Enthusiasm built as we met an old stray dog, climbed the mountain and drank sparkling water from the brook that ran down the middle section of the property. We began to catch a bit of Jack's vision. Our little family was very excited.

Family & Nanny Heidi

Shortly after our first trip to the mountain property, the Fitzgeralds decided to throw their hats into the ring with us. Anna and John dated back to Jack's Nutley days. After we married, they continued to count among our dearest friends. Our children had grown up together. We were excited that they would be able to live and work with us as pioneers in this new venture. John Fitzgerald and his earlier management experience overseeing production at the Johns Manville Company was a perfect balance to Jack's expansive salesman's approach to a new project.

Once the Frederick's property was under contract and our new company formed, Jack and John decided that they had better find out how to make snow. Both signed up and were hired to work at night as snowmakers at Snow Bowl, the small ski area in Jefferson Township. The job proved to be very physical. Each came home late every night, exhausted. The work involved moving around a fully-charged hose, which was attached to a charged air gun that was in turn blowing frozen water over a ski trail. The set-up was primitive but it did produce artificial snow. Jack and John insisted they often felt they were chasing large pythons that squirmed elusively away. They usually ended up covered with icy water and soaked to their long johns. Snowmaking, they learned, did not prompt one to give up one's day job! Their spirits remained undaunted, however, and at least they learned on the job the fundamentals of making snow in northern New Jersey.

With the Fitzgeralds aboard we could add a second piece to the project. With a deposit on the mountain site and a rough idea of how the mountain terrain could be forged into skiable slopes, if we were to grow from "them thar tow" to a legitimate ski area, we needed working space. Directly across from the Frederick site sat the Sussex Brush Company. This small company manufactured and distributed brushes. Its large sprawling building was being used for both offices and factory assembly. At that time, records show that the factory was run by Daisy Capparotto. Business was lagging and Daisy and her co-owners proved happy to sell. Now we had a place for a front office and a large storage area out back where we could keep the heavy equipment we needed to build and operate a ski area. Jack and I set up offices there to begin the marketing, public relations and communications operations. Another part of the building was partitioned off for accounting operations. This section housed a gigantic "computer" that was set up to do payroll and keep track of the bills to be paid. Our early prototype machine was very noisy and clunked along, but somehow got the job done.

Shortly after these two purchases, Jack and John gave notice to their employers and the two families moved to the mountain. In our earliest days while we were waiting for our own homes to be built on the mountain this meant sharing quarters in the old farmhouse. Later on in 1964 when we had moved into our chalet, John and Ann and their two children continued to live with us while their chalet was being built next door. We began to feel like Heidi in the Swiss Alps. The only thing missing was the cows with their bells being herded up the mountain in search of food and shelter. Meals were often hit-or-miss, but no one went hungry, and bedtime was always a big challenge. By the time we got all five kids to bed, we only had enough time leftover for a hand or two of bridge. Somehow the partnership and our friendship survived this test!

About this time, we decided that we needed a "barn burning" at the large

Frederick's barn. That space was needed to give way to building a proposed new base lodge. The local Vernon Volunteer Fire Department was happy to take on the job. They were rewarded with many barrels of beer and lots of hot dogs and hamburgers cooked on a large outdoor barbeque grill. We were rewarded on two fronts. The burning, which took place on August 19, 1963, won us a bit of understanding and reluctant approval from the locals. It also happened to be the author's birthday. Not only did the 1963 barn burning rank as one of the biggest events in town that year, it was by far my biggest birthday blaze ever.

Now we were ready to tackle site construction. After one or two meetings with the Vernon Township Planning Board, building permits were issued. It took all of two months to receive the necessary permits for the project to proceed. Today that same procedure would take a minimum of six years and would cost thousands of dollars of engineering, legal, environmental impact and traffic study fees. Town, county, state and federal approvals would be required. Back then life was far simpler and costs were low. A quart of milk cost 25 cents and a loaf of bread could be had for a dime.

With construction about to begin, we needed a bigger management team. Jack found two more partners to help. Once the other partners joined us, duties were divvied up according to perceived strengths. Jack, the born salesman, handled sales and marketing. John Fitzgerald, the level-headed personnel manager, oversaw site construction and later handled daily operations in the lodge and with the ski patrol. Matt Baker, the engineer, oversaw all things mechanical from snowmaking equipment to lift operations in his role as Equipment Maintenance, Lift, Snowmaking and Mountain Manager. Al Stasium, the accountant, took over the finances. It was quite a team.

Jack was always running around trying to keep the whole place moving forward and all the while working to attract skiers and bondholders to his dream mountain. As always, throughout the building stages, Jack had a compliment and a pat on the back for everyone from the janitor to the snowmakers and the parking lot attendants. It did not matter what their job was. He always told them they were doing a great job and thanked them for their efforts. Somehow, without a lot of fancy courses in personnel management techniques, he just naturally knew how to make his employees feel appreciated.

John Fitzgerald kept busy putting out fires and solving personnel problems. With the lodge nearing completion there was plenty of hiring that needed to be done to staff the lodge with restaurant personnel and inside workers, as well as countless other outside workers from lift attendants to security employees. He also busied himself interacting with the ski patrol and their needs to assure safety.

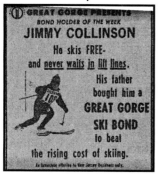

Al, in running the Accounting Department, wrestled daily with Jack over spending. Their discussions often came to a Mexican stand-off. Somehow or other, however, the money was found and construction moved forward.

Matt Baker's office in the rear of the brush factory was where the engineering designs for the lifts, snowmaking and sewerage disposal were laid out. Matt sought help from Curtis Wright, his former employer. Together they collaborated to design and install the 3,000 horsepower J65 Jet Engine that became the backbone of the extensive snowmaking capability required to cover the whole mountain.

With the realization that we needed professional guidance when it came to funding the project, Jack and Al met with financial planner, Walter Taradash. He recommended that we raise capital by selling "Ski Bonds". All the partners jumped into the challenge to generate buyers for the bonds. Bond holders were given lifetime skiing plus preferred lift lines on busy ski days. Many Sussex County residents purchased the bonds. Proceeds helped to cover costs until the ski area opened for business.

I have a very fond memory of Walter's gift to me when we last met. He was an avid gardener and especially loved the bearded Iris. I planted the four rhizomes Walter gave me in our yard in 1963. Since then have been separating Iris and sharing them with friends near and far. Some have been moved as far as Portland, Oregon where my niece has planted them in her garden. Walter's Iris have gone to Vermont, New York and North Carolina. Many have been planted on the golf course at Crystal Springs and friends have placed them in their Crystal Springs and Sparta home gardens. All they need is moderate watering and a nice sunny exposure. Contact my web site or go to Facebook in late spring if you would like to join in this Johnny Appleseed-like adventure with my and Walter's Iris. I would be so pleased to share them with you and hope you would also share them in the coming years.

Environmental standards then were not what they are now. Matt, however, recognized the need to plan for water and waste disposal, especially since water usage in snowmaking needed oversights. He contracted Dalton Shimko to design a sewage disposal system that would keep waste water clean enough to allow discharge dumping into the brook. Our clean mountain brook, flowed into Black Creek. From there this water moved on to Warwick, New York, then the Hudson River and from there into the Atlantic Ocean. Dalton, to his credit, anticipated some of the stricter controls that would someday plague developers. He was at the site daily, closely monitoring anything that affected his area of supervision.

The wives had a part, too. For the first ten years, Anna Fitzgerald ran the very successful Ski Shop. My duties quickly evolved into working full time running the Public Relations Department all while handling kids, doing housework, cooking meals and supervising homework. This was a challenging change from my earlier role as a stay-at-home mom. At least the commute to work was pretty easy. On snowy days if we could not drive down the steep road that led up the mountain to our chalet, we just slid down the mountain on a sled to the base lodge below.

Millie Baker became a registered Ski Patroller and Ellie Stasium started and ran a Great Gorge International Travel company at the area.

By the time we opened the area in 1965, the partners and their families, four couples and nine kids between them, were all living on the mountain in their own Tyrolean-style chalets. Each chalet was a unique creation of architect Sandy McIlvaine who had designed each to compliment his alpine-influenced base lodge. This combination of the base lodge and the mountain homes, as Jack used to say, were "BEE-YOOO-T-FUL". Living there also meant the partners were readily accessible whenever someone needed something. In season, that was often!

Looking back on these early beginnings, I wonder how we ever made it through these Camelot days. The other question that creeps in is… does disturbing this peaceful rural environment outweigh the gain in economic wealth and recreational benefits? My take today on our environmental impact is this: development always has a give and take. I still feel that the increased usage of the large tract of land which now encompasses all the recreation areas built here has, for the most part, not caused serious danger to the environment. We have provided a place where people can walk up the mountains in the summer and get away from the noise coming from the roads in the valley below. The sunsets during the late fall, winter and early spring are sensational. Every night the sky gives us a new show to enjoy. An old Swiss friend once said to me, "Enjoy! The best things in life are free." These things are still free and truly beautiful for everyone to enjoy. Many of yesterday's working farmers have left to enjoy the warmer climates in the Carolinas and points south. Other farms, with their compelling vistas, remain to balance the equation.

Happily, too, through-hikers on the Appalachian Trail still come down to Vernon to replenish their supplies. They often stay at the hostel at St. Thomas Church. There they enjoy a hot shower, a clean cot and often a good breakfast in the church social hall. When the hikers climb back onto the trail they stand a moment on Lookout Point to enjoy the beauty of the fields and farm houses of the valley before continuing on their way. Occasionally, friends have asked us to provide lodging to give hikers a break after months on the trail. We give them a shower and bathroom facilities, a place to shave and do their laundry, and then take them for a good dinner at the George Inn in McAfee. They usually leave early the next morning to get back on the trail. We think they leave with warm feelings about our little Sussex County niche in the upper corner of New Jersey.

So, yes, I feel the benefits of usage for recreation outweighs its negative environmental impact!

Jack accepting award from JCP&L for work done at Stone Hill condos

– CHAPTER 5 –

GREAT GORGE GETS ITS NAME

Once construction on the new ski area began, everyone involved had suggestions for what the new project should be named. Every ski area in Vermont, New Jersey, Pennsylvania and New York State had a name its owners felt best-suited its unique character. Since ours was to be the largest ski area in New Jersey, we knew this demanded a name suggesting a BIG MOUNTAIN CHARACTER.

During our earliest days of planning back in our Lake Valhalla living room, friends threw out ideas focusing on mountains, valleys, snow bowls, creeks and gorges. We decided to wait until we moved to the area and could really sense the true character of the drama we were rapidly beginning to live.

From the first, Jack worked with topographic maps and began to fit imagined trails to the terrain the maps showed. He soon realized, however, he needed some expert advice to modify and improve upon his design. Jack hired one of the top ski trail designers in the country, Otto Schneibs, to do some consulting. Schneibs had designed trails at a number of popular areas in the United States including Sun Valley, Belleayre, White Face and Bristol Mountain.

Once Schneibs arrived at the site, he and Jack spent a busy week walking the mountain, testing ideas. The stray dog whom we met the day Jack introduced us to his mountain hung around and accompanied them on their morning explorations. Each afternoon the two men crowded into the old farmhouse that, at the time, was also the site of the temporary sales office and is now the current ski patrol building. They worked and reworked the topographic maps. They hung these maps on the walls of the crowded little house and debated each new change – all while the stray dog patiently watched. When Otto Schneibs and Jack were testing trail designs, dozens of other salesmen were around trying to land contracts to build lifts or install the electric and snowmaking systems. A lift salesman named "Otto" and another named "Boris" were the most persistent of the lot. Our newly adopted stray dog was probably confused when addressed as "Otto" when the salesman Boris was around and then called "Boris" when the salesman Otto was at the site. When the final lift contracts were awarded to Boris Vilhar, our dog officially inherited the name Otto. Otto Weber, who was not awarded the lift contract in 1965, probably never heard of this little charade that went on behind his back. Perhaps he will learn of it now. This story should also clarify that it was he, rather than Otto Schneibs, for whom our mountain dog was named.

After visiting us for a week, Otto Schneibs' business called him elsewhere. Jack stepped up his own efforts, fortified by the tricks of the trade he had learned from the wise old pioneer in ski area construction. During these days Jack enjoyed keeping the canine Otto close at hand as he continued his daily oversight of trail construction, elevations, excavations and a variety of other design problems. Pioneers in ski area design rarely have previous experience. They sense feasible layouts by walking them out in the field. Amazingly, for a novice designer, most of the trails Jack laid out still exist as he originally designed them in 1963-1964. Of course, some minor changes were made as the area grew, new terrain was opened and new lifts were added. Clearly, however, the experience Jack gained in fitting the Great Gorge needs to the limits of its terrain was most beneficial when in 1994, some thirty years later, he began designing Black Bear Golf Course.

Harry Hicks, the area's first contracted publicist, has a humorous recollection of these early days. Jack had told Harry he needed a brochure to help explain what a potential skier/investor could only imagine when gazing upward from the street below at the site where the base lodge was to go. Harry found an experienced New York City artist who made the long trek out from the city for an on-site inspection of what he needed to draw to showcase what was still only a gleam in the designer's eye. Jack expansively flung out an arm in a direction to the right. "There," he enthused, "there's the beginner trail we'll be cutting next week. Make that look gentle. And, over there," he emoted, "we'll be having the steepest vertical drop this side of Vermont. Make that blue!" His partner, John Fitzgerald, standing nearby sweeping his arm in contrast to the left, could be heard, correcting, "But, Jack, you told us the beginner area was going there and the steep expert trail was up there on the right!" Objections sustained. A trail map was drawn and printed and future skiers honed their skills on trails well-suited to their abilities. This same artist and public relations advisor also asked us for a name to use to get the word out about the coming new area.

Ann & John Fitzgerald, Flossie Zemac & Joe Dean

Upon hearing Jack talk about the mountain's wonderful and rather distinctive gorge that would help funnel skiers, beginner and expert alike, more quickly down the mountain all the while exposing them to a very distinctive run-off, a friend had suggested "Great Gorge" as a fitting name. This name was still in the rather tentative-choice category, but our publicists needed something immediately. So, almost as a test, they started using it for our earliest brochures.

Any question we might have had about the appropriateness of the selection of Great Gorge as a name ended when the installation of the Kamikaze Lift was completed. In the fall of 1966 the engineers had applied the finishing touches to our attractive new expert area. The newest lift had its towers encased in sturdy cement, its cable strung, and its chairs hanging, awaiting their call to duty. Matt Baker, in his role as chief engineer in charge of safety and quality control, needed to test the new system. He asked Anna Fitzgerald and me to be the first women to ride the lift. We were very excited about this "maiden voyage". Once we settled into one of the chairs, we noticed it had no safety bar to hold us in if a problem arose. It was too late for us to bail out of this harrowing adventure, however.

Matt started the lift from the bottom and off we went. He knew exactly when we would be over the highest point halfway up the lift ride. In a playful mood, Matt stopped the lift abruptly, leaving us swinging out in open space. We were hanging and swaying over the deep ravine below. We were terrified. What we knew from the ground as a gorge was, from this perspective, a gigantic crevice below us. We hugged each other and began praying that we would not be pitched out of the chair. Need I add that safety bars were put in several weeks later?

The terrain below us that day had always been called the Gorge. After that terrifying initial ride all other name choices for the area were off the board. Great Gorge it was and so it remained as long as we operated The Great Gorge Ski Area. Thus inspired, the name Great Gorge had a very powerful and rather ominous ring which continued to set the tone for visitors over the years. People frequently asked where the Great Gorge was. We always replied that they had to take a ride up lift #3 to see this great chasm for themselves. The name, like the gorge itself, was all part of our "BIG MOUNTAIN" mystique. A little bit of subliminal public relations was at work here.

We settled on Great Gorge as our name of choice and it proved to be a rich and versatile name that seemed to attract attention. Harry Hicks, our marketing and public relations consultant, wrote Great Gorge radio ads to help popularize our area's new name. This early radio ad, used extensively around Presidents' Week in 1965, is one of his more whimsical and creative efforts:

The following is a Public Service message, researched by Harry C. Hicks, to honor our Founding Father.

George Washington had little formal schooling, had difficulty writing, and never mastered the art of spelling. On occasions, he signed his name G O R G E. In spite of his limited mastery of written communications, people described him with one word: GREAT.

He taught himself a good deal about mathematics. By the time he was 14 he had become a professional surveyor. At age 16 he was given a job charting vast wilderness properties of a distant relative, Lord Fairfax. This led to his appointment as the official surveyor of Culpepper County. Because of his wilderness training, the young map-maker was then made a lieutenant colonel by Governor Dunwiddie of Virginia. He was sent on an expedition to chart and record the forts being built by the French along the Ohio River, an action that counts as one of the first of the French and Indian War.

Next a friendly Indian guide asked Colonel Washington to survey the hills of McAfee, New Jersey and "Great George", as he was known, obliged. Great George made his way to the Port Authority Bus Terminal and took an Intercity Bus from Platform #124 at 8:30 AM. He was in McAfee without delay.

With the aid of his Indian guide, a legitimate Indian, Great George planted tobacco and catnip and harvested most of the trees from a hill in McAfee. His intent was to plant Christmas trees every two years as a form of crop rotation (and to sell them wholesale to local fire departments). A base lodge was constructed from native timber.

During his first winter in New Jersey, while collecting firewood for his wife, he was balancing two flat trees on his head, and he slipped – all the way down the vertical drop of 1,033 feet. George decided that he must put safety ropes along the path to prevent future falls, and Martha, being a compulsively neat housekeeper, soon began washing her canvas chairs and hanging them on those ropes to dry.

During the miserable winter of 1777 Great George had his first good year of the sport he invented – wood slipping. Riding up the slopes on Martha's canvas chairs, he would slide down from the summit on the thin trees he had harvested.

One day in 1873, after his army had been dismissed, Great George settled down in the new cocktail lounge. He listened to Dottie Stalwarth at the piano playing her swinging Dixie Melodies, and contemplated his desire for public life. There were difficulties between the States and the Thirteen Colonies were not united satisfactorily. In 1788 a convention was called. Wine and chili-dogs were served, a constitution was written which would bring the states together, and as he toasted his buns by one of the big walk-in fireplaces in the base lodge, Washington was called upon to be made President.

The rest, of course, is known to all of us. The importance of regular, out-door exercise as a means of maintaining health, relieving stress and developing potential talents is accepted by today's medical authorities.

You may not be able to be a gentleman farmer, but the next time you want to "get away from it all", enjoy the experience of Great Gorge. It's good for your constitution.

Once we had settled on a name for our area, we needed a logo to make it more readily recognizable. Dalton Shimko was one of our early employees and a man of many talents. Not only did he check the sewerage plant frequently each day to be sure all the health requirements were met, in his spare moments he used his artistic talents to come up with the "GG" design of the letters ending in two skis facing each other that we adapted for our advertising logo. His logo was ever popular, too, on the ski patches and pins our skiers proudly wore.

Naming lifts, trails and other parts of our mountain complex also added a bit of creative fun to all the daily frustrations of smoothly meshing the many parts of our new area. Once we decided on being Great Gorge, we still needed plenty of other names.

Our partners got a bit of fame when it came to naming trails. Beginner skiers could practice turns in "Baker's Field" that went from mid-station down the top part of the lower mountain area. Once lifts ran to the top of the mountain, the most popular way down was known as "Jumping Jack." Jack always said that was his favorite trail, but the trail's name was also an apt description of his busy ways. Trails were also named for the other two partners, Fitz's Folly for John Fitzgerald, and Al's Alley in honor of Al Stasium.

Early on, the trail name that folks remembered best and the one that created the most buzz was the expert "Kamikaze" trail, so named to suggest suicide for any novice skier who ventured on to it before their skills could keep them in control.

Later, when it came to naming trails, a rather amusing story about the significance of our selection of Kamikaze as a name for our expert trail comes to mind:

One day three teenage girls were standing and quivering while they stood at the top of Kamikaze, afraid to venture down this advanced trail. They headed over to the new Arndt's Delight trail which ran parallel to Kamikaze. That sounded as though it might be a little easier, but it really was not. A ski patrolman noticed the whole situation and asked the girls if they needed his help. The girls explained that they felt they would "get killed" going down that trail. The patrolman answered: "If you go down Arndt's here, you are going to get more than killed." He applied a bit of Yankee ingenuity there and no doubt saved the patrol from some extra toboggan work that day. As the story was later retold, the girls took off their skis and slid down to the base on their fannies and were not even bruised.

In the first season of full operation, a 3,500-foot double chairlift serviced the Kamikaze trail, located on the south of the steepest side of the mountain. The gentler slopes on the northern side of our mountain were serviced by two

1,200-foot chairlifts. Skiers slid off the first lift and, if they wanted to go up higher, after a few steps they boarded the second lift for a ride to our "Mid Mountain" section. Lacking more descriptive names, these first two chairs were dubbed #1 and #2. The Kamikaze lift was called #3. The lift offering transportation from the base to the top of the mountain that was installed several years later was rightfully called the "Summit Lift".

Numbering or naming lifts was done for efficiently and accuracy. For safety reasons, having designated lifts helped the Ski Patrol communicate more accurately whenever they were needed quickly. Lifts also needed names to speed help in cases of emergency breakdowns.

A 500-foot t-bar also was built to service some trails near the #3 area which did not have heavy usage. It primarily served rank beginners. I do not remember ever using that lift or it having a name, but the records show it was there. During our first year of operation we also had a short platter pull or puma lift which was installed on the beginners' slope in the Sammis cornfield, property we leased for a season from the neighboring family. This tow took up some initial slack, but we soon found it easier to operate on our own property. The use of the Sammis name ended there.

Happily for our story, this and our other marketing efforts soon made the name Great Gorge a part of the greater New York area's vocabulary, synonymous with winter fun.

38

Peg Skiing

Louis Schflaginger Trick Skiing

– CHAPTER 6 –

FLUSHING MEADOWS PROVIDES A BIT OF INTERNATIONAL FLAIR

Architect's drawing of 1st Lodge at Great Gorge

The new ski area was beginning to take shape outdoors and groundbreaking work had started on the proposed base lodge. Another problem loomed. How do we take care of the skiers when they are not outside skiing up and down the mountain? How can we furnish our fancy new base lodge without breaking the bank?

We had already hired the highly regarded architect Sandy McIlvaine to design the lodge at Great Gorge. Sandy was well known for his innovative architectural artistry at Stratton Mountain in Manchester, Vermont and Squaw Valley in Olympic Valley, California. As part of his contract with us, Sandy also designed all of the chalets which were being built on the upper slopes of Hamburg Mountain. His lovely architectural creations gave an alpine feel to the entire project. Making the base lodge and the mountain housing seem like pictures out of the Swiss Alps gave both an especially charming effect. Most of the housing being built at this time in Sussex County was of a low-cost bi-level "vinyl Williamsburg" style. This may have filled the need for affordable housing, but it lacked the beautiful design needed to preserve the bucolic charm of the area.

In 1964-1965 the New York World's Fair was held in New York City's Corona Park in Flushing Meadows, a site in the park adjacent to today's National Tennis Center and the host of one of tennis' premier events, the US Open Championship. The "aha" moment came when Jack read that all the structures used for the World's Fair were to be sold and removed.

Jack made some inquiries and subsequently met with the owners of the lovely alpine building that housed the Swiss Pavilion. The building, constructed in chalet style, with its Swiss art, architecture and furnishings was just what was needed to give our budding ski area an aura of authenticity.

The Fair is well remembered for its aerial tram cars that passed overhead throughout the day. A futile attempt was made to purchase the tramway, but that proved well beyond what we could afford.* The Swiss Pavilion would, however, answer our prayers for obtaining suitable furnishings and equipment at a cost more fitting to our budget. Our beautiful but empty new lodge,

---

*I know Jack would have loved to get his hands on that tramway. It most likely was the inspiration he had later in 1971 for building a tramway from Great Gorge to the Playboy Hotel. That cherished dream of his has yet to become a reality.

---

now under construction, could use all the contents of the Pavilion. The Pavilion's furniture fit perfectly with the décor of a ski lodge. Behind the scenes we needed help, too. The final agreement we negotiated allowed us to purchase all the pavilion's permanent fixtures from latrines and sinks to its kitchen equipment and storage freezers. The savings proved phenomenal.

When the Fair closed in late 1965, Jack and John rounded up a number of local men who owned trucks to go with them to Flushing Meadows. Included in this crew were our farm neighbors, Leo and Lenny Sammis. At this time only union workers were allowed into Flushing Meadows. Sorties to the site had to be made after dark.

Once there, our crew of moonlighting workers dismantled the contents of the Pavilion and the structure itself. Disconnecting all the plumbing proved one of the most difficult jobs of all. Every night for two weeks the crew went in with crow bars, chain saws and whatever else was needed to get the Pavilion and its contents out of there. A few World's Fair security people were happy to receive a nice-sized tip to allow our motley group onto the premises. Amazingly, no one was arrested and things went smoothly.

Once cleared for hauling, everything that was movable was packed as securely as possible into the farm trucks and driven to New Jersey. Safely back home in Sussex County, most of the haul was unloaded either at the old Frederick's farmhouse or stored across the street at the new company headquarters in the old Sussex Brush Company. Until they could be put to further use, the remnants of the Pavilion's wooden siding, flooring and glass were stored on a nearby Sussex Borough farm where the excited local farmer was happy to be part of this local history in the making.

Work on the base lodge progressed. With John Fitzgerald, who had previous experience in construction, in charge supervising, things were accomplished in record time. All of the Pavilion's cafeteria, kitchen and rest-room

Bar furnishings at Great Gorge from the Swiss Pavilion

fixtures found a new home in our base lodge. Amazingly, even the large windows of the Swiss Pavilion proved to be an unexpected bonus. Most of the Pavilion's large glass windows were re-cut and adapted to fit as windows for the new lodge. The remaining wood, walls and roof materials could also be adapted for use in our building in various other ways.

Most of the Pavilion's dining room fixtures and its furniture went to the room in the lodge which was later named The Barn Stube. The Barn Stube became Great Gorge's highly popular restaurant, featuring terrific Austrian, German and Swiss dishes. Adding to its ambience, at this point in construction The Barn Stube's walls were being made from old barn wood. In our case the wood we used was that salvaged from the old barn that had once stood on the Frederick's Farm. The remnants of the barn on Jack's original purchase had earlier been "burned" to make way for our new base area site. Wisely, all the usable barn siding had been set aside before the Vernon volunteer firemen took over. With similar foresight in the case of the transported Swiss Pavilion, we eventually incorporated its remaining wood, walls and roof materials in other parts of our two buildings. What we finally could not use, our local farmer happily kept for his future needs.

Another of the treasures that came out of our Swiss Pavilion purchase was the large cow bell given to us by the Swiss gentleman who had previously owned the Pavilion. We mounted that near the slope-side door of the building and clanged it on several special occasions.

Visitors to the base lodge also commented favorably on a number of large oil paintings by the artist Victor Ruzo. Not only had Ruzo been the architect of the Fair's Swiss Pavilion, he had also been commissioned to paint alpine portraits to depict life on farms, in meadows and on mountains with people dressed in national holiday attire to brighten the walls of the Pavillion. As part of Jack's negotiations, these paintings now had a home in McAfee, New Jersey. A few examples of these works are reproduced here in the *Memory Lane* section of this book. Over the years other artists visited the area to paint some of our most picturesque scenes. Adding their work to our walls made an attractive addition to our Ruzo paintings.

Putting all the furniture and fixtures to such good use at Great Gorge was wonderful. The stars were indeed in alignment in 1965. It was too bad that the stars did not stay in alignment during some of the warm winters to come and also that other factors ultimately brought an end to the dream created at Great Gorge.

1967 Watercolor of Great Gorge skiing
(Color prints available at Kurlynj@gmail.com)

– CHAPTER 7 –

THE MOUNTAIN MEN AND OUR OTHER SPECIAL HELPERS

Help Wanted... New ski area under construction looking for strong male employees who are willing to work flexible hours in all types of weather conditions, are capable of lifting 200+ pounds and can work with other men in a mountain setting. Must be willing to accept minimum wage if without skills. Room for advancement if willing to learn how to handle electric wires, water pipes and loud noise, have waterproof boots and clothing, are willing to work days or nights and sometimes both. Applicants with skills in handling tractors, plows, engine repairs and some experience in farm work especially needed. This could easily have been used when Great Gorge management began hiring "Mountain Men" for the new ski area in McAfee.

Finding help was not a problem. Happily the many Sussex County farms that surrounded us proved to be an important source of supply for help. We literally recruited these hearty workers from our own backyard. Local farm workers who needed work during the non-growing season became the core of our Mountain Men. Most had already had years of experience operating and fixing farm machinery. To them, a faltering ski lift or snow gun seemed pretty much like a broken tractor.

Since Jack and John had taken jobs at the Snow Bowl Ski Area in order to learn all they could about snowmaking, they worked when the weather was favorable for snowmaking – which was almost every night. As snowmakers they learned how to wrestle with heavy hoses, pipes and couplings. Large wrenches became standard equipment. They learned how to mix the water and the air which were necessary for making light, man-made snow. Survival every night depended on their enthusiasm for learning this new skill which they needed for their new endeavor.

Every organization has a few employees who stand out from the rest. These employees are ready for any or all unforeseen problems or emergencies. They can be depended upon to respond quickly to whatever is asked of them. The Great Gorge Mountain Men were all that and more. We soon learned that they could be counted on to get the job done, not always professionally, but always with a zest and a ready will to keep things running. Whenever a lift malfunctioned or the snowmaking mix was not producing, they proved resourceful, as well as fearless. This type of hardy employee was especially valuable for work in the unforgiving environment of a project such as Great Gorge that relied so completely on snow for its daily existence.

Jack and John knew the rigors of the mountain demanded skill and patience, and often guts and brawn. These qualities proved especially valuable during our construction phase. We also needed helicopters to build the ski lifts. Using helicopters to hoist massive steel towers and place the lift towers in formed cement exactly as the area designers specified was a test for the best of our men. This job was often muddy and sometimes dangerous. Just envision, the work involved in fitting miles of air and water pipes to the rough terrain of trails that ran through the woods. Add to that the miles of electric wires needed to keep the electricity running smoothly and safely. Thankfully, we did not have any major accidents during the construction phase at Great Gorge.

Later, once we were up and running, we asked the men to work longer hours. Their job as snowmakers involved setting up and moving snow guns. Their workday was not finished until the last slope was cleared of skiers and the slopes were covered and groomed for another day of skiing. Each day, after the skiers left the mountain, Mountain Men in Sno-Cats began grooming the trails. Early on, we closed for the day at 4:00pm and trail grooming began. Pretty soon, we closed down to groom but re-opened three nights a week for night skiing and another round of grooming. To extend the skiing day and handle our growing crowds, the mountain eventually operated every night. Growing numbers of school buses pulled into the area every afternoon filled with students headed for the lodge to boot up for their twilight or nighttime adventure. Many of our skiers went to their city jobs during the day and then drove to the mountain for the joy of skiing at night. These extra hours of skiing meant, in turn, that still more Mountain Men had to be added to the payroll.

Today these loyal Great Gorge employees would be considered poster boys for the country's work force. Their transition from summer to winter was done smoothly every year. Mountain Men never collected unemployment for 18 months or asked for an additional 18-month extension. When one season ended, they found work elsewhere. They worked on local farms, ran the local gas stations or joined the booming construction industry which was beginning to flourish. During the years our Great Gorge Zoo operated, a few men even doubled as zoo attendants. They surely would have put a dent in today's high unemployment rate.

Chief among our valuable Mountain Men was the Mountain Manager, Charlie O'Brien. Charlie was a burly, red-faced Irishman known for his good humor, as well as his decisiveness. As you might expect, he was also a very colorful character. We came to appreciate his willingness to put his all into his job. If snow needed to be made all night long, Charlie was always on hand, never willing to ask his men to work longer or harder than he. This type of loyalty endeared him to his workers and enabled him to hire good men, men like Wacky Joe Mazur, so named for his ability to go hand-over-hand down the lift cables and towers, Big Al, Russ, and a fourth equally memorable employee known only as "Indian".

The stories that accumulated while Charlie worked for us are legend. The local cops loved Charlie so much that escapades that took place "under the influence" often went unchallenged. A particular favorite concerns his rather proprietary handling of a delivery man who failed to recognize the importance of his job of keeping our ski mountain in top working order.

On this particular day, Charlie desperately needed a part for a lift that was down. He waited impatiently for the UPS man to bring the part. When the UPS man arrived at the Administration Building, no one in Administration had the money needed to pay for the part. The UPS guy got back in his truck and headed back out of town with the part. When Charlie heard about it, in a rage he called the cops to help and went to the bar to take out his frustration. Next thing he knew, there were the cops happily escorting the UPS driver back to the ski area. A million similar stories like that about Charlie still make the rounds.

Charlie had one habit which I did not always appreciate. Every St. Patty's

Day he began his celebrations early in the morning. Later, he would quietly sneak up to our chalet and, more often than not, lure Snowflake, our beautiful white cat out the front door. There were no such things as locks on our home. With kids and friends popping in day and night, locks made no sense. Once in Charlie's clutches, Snowflake was then transformed into a true Irish cat, carefully died green with vegetable dye. Snowflake slunk around the rest of the day wondering why he looked so different from his fellow mountain cats. In true cat fashion, Snowflake would appear next morning all cleaned up after a night of licking the sweet-flavored coloring. Perhaps Charlie, feeling a bit of remorse, came back to assist in the cat bath? Who knows for sure? What we do know is that if you are ever tempted to match Charlie's antics, don't!

GG Mountain Men & Zoo attendants on Pulaski fire truck with lion snuggled next to Charlie O'Brien

My favorite picture from our Great Gorge days appears here in this book. It shows Charlie O'Brien with his star Mountain Men perched on a fire truck. The truck was purchased from the Pulaski Fire Department in nearby Pulaski, New York, and it was a classic. Note the young lion cub, a Mountain Men mascot and a member of our zoo family, who can also be seen here sprawled on the fire engine.

Among the guys shown in the photo are three of the original Mountain Men, "Wackie", "Indian" and Russ. Wackie, whose real name is Joe, still works summers at Crystal Springs Resort where he runs the Crystal Springs Golf Club cart yard. In the winter months, Joe gets away to Florida.

To digress a bit further about our Mountain Men, we should add a few words more words about the kind of help we "city folk" found when we went looking. From the beginning, some of our best workers were only as far as next door, waiting for us at the Sammis Farm. Most of the farms in our area were dairy farms. Several others grew crops, most notably corn. Our immediate neighbors, the Sammis family – Gloria and Leo, and Delores and Lenny, were noted for their specialty, Luther Hill corn.

If you have never had Luther Hill corn, you have missed a masterpiece of consistently good flavor. Sammis' Luther Hill was particularly outstanding.

Leo and Lenny Sammis, and their seasonal help took care of the fields while Gloria and Delores ran their food stand on Route 94. In season, we usually purchased at least a dozen ears a day. If you were looking for the best corn, this was the place to come. The Sammis stand was equally popular with locals and vacationers alike. Their Luther Hill corn was the best we "city folk" had ever had.

We never minded the annual spraying of their fields. Come spring, having small crop-duster planes zoom across the farm was a frequent occurrence. As each plane went down the field, it lifted quickly just before flying over our house. What excitement for our "Mountain Kids" whenever the crop dusters flew by for a visit.

The Sammis farmland is still there today, although most of it is no longer cultivated. The newest Great Gorge owners are reported to be planning a large recreation facility on land adjacent to the Sammis Farm. Permits to build are pending approval but, as of this writing, have not yet been issued.

Early on, as a reward for our long hours of hard work, we treated ourselves to a special perk. Sometimes, after hours, the Kurlander, Fitzgerald, Baker and Stasium families took over the use of a lift and one trail in the lower end of the mountain just for themselves. We usually skied on Monday nights when the area was closed. Once the lodge was closed up for the day, one of the Mountain Men would turn on the lift and lights again just so the area families could ski on their own private turf. Usually, one of the ski patrolmen stayed after hours to see that we were safe. How we cherished an hour or two set aside just for family skiing at our own private area. Sometimes other people would drive by and stop to see if they could join the festivities. This special treat, however, was reserved just for the families who had put so much of their lives and energies into making Great Gorge a reality.

Ski patrol members were another very important part of the skiing scene at Great Gorge, as they are at hundreds of ski areas throughout the United States. Most patrollers were, and continue to be, volunteers. All of them are trained in first aid and emergency responses and are proficient in skiing. Patrollers spend many hours practicing their skills, lifting the injured to a sled, and then skillfully transporting them to the warmth of the patrol room for further evaluation. Usually the injuries are minor, although we have seen our share of more serious situations. Not only do patrollers provide invaluable assistance to skiers who are injured, they help enforce safety. No area could survive without their great contribution to help ensure that skiers have a safe and enjoyable experience.

The contributions made by our patrollers were no exception. Our patrollers, led by Geroge Kabash, were all members of the National Ski Patrol. They lived by the same high standards that the national organization demands. They prided themselves on their quick response to any and all emergencies. Our ski patrollers credited the walkie-talkie communication system they had set up using Motorola radios as one factor in their ability to be on the spot so quickly.

Our ski patrol was never just made up of male volunteers. Female ski patrollers at the Gorge were also volunteers who worked most weekdays, performing all the duties of a patrolman. Like their male counterparts, one of their functions was to be on duty at the patrol shack at the top of the mountain. If there was an injury on one of the trails, they could quickly get their skis on and ski down to help the injured person until a toboggan was brought on the scene.

Ski Patrol gang –

Chicken Legs John Murray, Dannis Fielding, Dave Dunning

The girls in the Patrol – Jane, Sandy, Lilly

The gals on the ski patrol, however, went the guys one better and added an extra feminine touch to the job. Some of the best times at the patrol shack were during lunch. While they waited for a radio call to assist a skier, talk among patrollers raved about who could provide the most luscious dishes, not of the "Bunny" variety. The gals soon began upstaging the men's less elaborate contributions, taking turns bringing in wonderful soups, sandwiches, home-made cookies and hot beverages to share with patrollers on duty. These extra social touches instituted by the patrol "ladies" knit the group even tighter. At the core of this group were Sandy Larsen, Jane Pier, Charlotte Plath and Millie Baker. Most of them had kids still in school. They volunteered on a part-time basis and were most often assigned on Mondays.

The best the guys could do as a concession to superior culinary skill was to give their fellow patrollers their "day". They happily began referring to Monday as "PTA Mondays", derived from the better known Parent Teachers Association. While they pretended that volunteering to work on PTA Mondays was only an entry-level job at the bottom rung of the ladder, several patrolmen were caught trying to wrangle a Monday assignment that promised a lunch upgrade in exchange for a bit of swallowed pride.

Many of our patrollers still also recall our patrol's most amazing happening. One day, a 26 year old male skier walked into the lodge with a ski pole stuck into his abdomen. He had fallen getting off the #1 lift and walked down the trail and into the lodge with the ski pole still impaled in his stomach. John Fitzgerald spotted him and quickly escorted him to the Ski Patrol Building. An ambulance was called and he was transported to one of the hospitals located a few miles from Great Gorge. The skier survived.

The role played by Luis Schafflinger and his fellow Austrians in our ski school was another very important contribution to the success of our new ski area and also needs special mention here. Over the years, thousands of new skiers took their first learn-to-ski lesson at Great Gorge. Thanks to Luis and his exceptionally talented teachers, these rank beginners soon turned into "real skiers". The Austrians in the Ski School helped teach all of us the classic style they advocated and executed with such class and ease.

The first day of skiing for beginners always seemed to be a struggle. After a few visits to Great Gorge, they began to improve and soon were enjoying most of the trails. We became a gateway ski area for skiers who learned from us and later took their passion on to bigger or more distant areas in Vermont and Colorado. They never forgot, however, how much they learned from the instructors who helped them develop their skills.

We continued to think of all our area employees – our Mountain Men, our ski patrollers and our ski school instructors, as family. They, in turn, supported us in our goal of giving the area a family feel. This same family atmosphere at the Gorge continued to exist for many years. Skiing families were thrilled to have their own special a place in New Jersey where they could enjoy challenging skiing while also spending hours or days happily savoring sunsets filtering over our snowy slopes, experiencing the quiet of soft drifting snow or simply discovering the ever-changing beauty of Hamburg Mountain. Our good friend, Robert Gerber, said it best. Before pointing his skis down the mountain, he would sometimes stop to look around, take a moment to reflect on the beauty he saw and repeat his favorite words of wisdom: "The best things in life are free." When you take the time to reflect on that simple statement, you too can catch the essence of being there to experience the joy of skiing and the beauty of the mountain and the valley below.

Standing one evening waiting for the family to join me, I overheard a conversation taking place in the lift overhead between two people riding quietly up the mountain. A man was exclaiming to his friend that this was "just like being in the Alps". I chuckled when hearing that, thinking of the concrete of the city they left behind in exchange for a lovely day at the mountain. The skiers spoke "Americanese" with a little Brooklyn accent. Their conversation suggested that for a few hours they too were no longer city dwellers but had become a part of our Great Gorge family.

Lift Rates:

(Children — To Age 14)

Weekends and Holidays:

	Adults	Children
All Day, All Lifts	$7.00	$5.00
Half Day, All Lifts	5.00	4.00
Beginners' Area (Rope Tow &Platter Pull only) All Day	5.00	4.00
Beginners' Area, Half Day	4.00	3.00

Weekdays:

	Adults	Children
All Day, All Lifts	$5.00	$4.00
Half Day, All Lifts	4.00	3.00
Beginners' Area, All Day	4.00	3.00
Beginners' Area Half Day	3.00	2.00

Night Skiing:

Tuesday through Sunday	$4.50	$3.50

Twilight Skiing: (3:00 to 11:00 P. M.)

Tuesday through Friday	$5.50	$4.50

Season Pass Rates:

	Adults	Children
Unlimited Season Pass (For all lifts — days, nights, weekends and holidays)	$125	$90
Night Skiing Season Pass (Night skiing only)	$50	$35
Weekday Season Pass (Monday through Friday, days only, including holidays)	$65	$55
Weekday and Night Season Pass (Monday through Friday and all nights includ. holidays)	$75	$65

GREAT GORGE

SKI AREA, McAFEE, N. J. Tel. 827-9146

Season Pass Rates:

Family Season Pass Rates
(Applicable toward Unlimited Season Pass only)
Restricted to members of the same family

Adults	$125
Children (to age 14)	90
Each Additional Adult	100
Each Additional Child	65

A 10% Discount will be given if pass is paid in one payment, on or before October 15, 1967.

Ski School Rates:

LUIS SCHAFFLINGER SKI SCHOOL

Class Lessons (10 A. M. to Noon & 2 P. M. to 4 P. M.)	$ 4.50
Eight Lesson Book	30.00
Private Lesson (Individual — day or nights)	10.00
Each additional person	5.00

HANSL & GRETL SKI KLASSE

Children Ages 2 to 6
9:30 - Noon; 1:30 - 4:00 Daily $3.00 per session
Equipment, instruction, refreshments and games included.

(All prices subject to change without notice)

Ski Rentals:

Wooden Skis, Poles, Boots	$5.50
Head Skis, Poles, Boots	6.50
Wooden Skis and Poles	4.50
Head Skis and Poles	5.50
Poles	1.00
Boots	2.00
Wooden Skis	3.50
Head Skis	4.50

3% Sales Tax on Rental Equipment.

Deposit and car registration required on all rentals.

– CHAPTER 8 –

OTTO MOUNTAIN DOG

The first day that Jack took the family to see "his" Hamburg Mountain, we met Otto. Otto was a large mixed-breed collie, distinguished by his very full mane and an imperfectly formed right front leg that caused his paw to splay. As a local veterinarian explained later, either Otto was born with rickets or he suffered poor nutrition as a puppy. Either way, his gimpy paw gave him a very distinctive limp. Early on, he tried to hide behind this rather abused look, but we all immediately loved him. Surprisingly, no one we asked had any idea where he came from or who was his rightful owner. From the day we met him, then and ever after, he was our mountain dog.

From day one, Otto appeared to like us, too. Once negotiations for the purchase of the Frederick Farm were complete and we had taken ownership of the property we proposed to turn into a ski area, we were on site every day. Although not included in the transfer deed, somehow Otto came along with the property. He was quick to let us know he was ready for adoption. He particularly appeared to enjoy his role of helping Jack supervise construction work at the site. Eventually his duties increased and our friendly dog could be seen greeting skiers, truck drivers, policemen or anyone else who came to visit his mountain home. No guest was meant to feel unwanted even when on rare occasions that guest turned out to be the local dog catcher dispatched to guarantee him a permanent home.

During our early days at the mountain site as construction began and potential investors wanted to view the upper reaches of the mountain, Jack and his new canine friend needed a means to get around the mountain. As luck would have it, the Fitzgerald family still owned an old army-issue green Jeep that badly needed a new muffler. Years before, the Fitzgeralds had used the Jeep as a utilitarian second car before they retired it to their Pines Lake garage. Since budgetary constraints dictated few purchases of new equipment, the Fitzgerald Jeep could be given a second life. The resurrected vehicle continued to need a new muffler but it ran! Transported to Vernon, its distinctive bangs caused only a minimum stir in its mountain setting. Since it never left the site, it never did have a proper license plate. Happily, though, Jack and Otto were now mobile.

When Jack turned the Jeep on in the morning, complete with full noisy banging, Otto wakened from his overnight nap and began to bark. He gleefully followed the Jeep all over the mountain. He could be seen happily running alongside the Jeep, barking with delight. If Otto looked particularly tired, Jack invited him to jump in and ride along.

From the very first day skiers arrived on site, Otto developed his own fan club. Everyone fell in love with him. Children hugged and petted him. Adults gave him gentle pats on the head or sometimes a dog biscuit treat. He enjoyed every minute of this attention.

Little snacks gleaned here and there from the kitchen chef or the customers kept Otto well supplied with food throughout the day. He used the "guilt" approach. He would test out his sense of smell and hone in on the table with the most appealing repast. Otto would then sit down beside the snacking skiers and quietly let them know he, too, would enjoy sharing a bite of their meal. He thrived on this diet. I do not think we ever bought a bag of dog food. Certainly, we never concerned ourselves with offering the well-balanced diets urged on pet owners today.

Otto also never lost his zest or his ability to sniff out the action. He had several favorite routines. When skiers began arriving in the morning, he hung out around the base area in front of the lodge. He willingly gave a lick to anyone who offered a hand or felt the need to give him a hug. Later in the day, if the action waned down below, he summoned his energy and could be seen running up and down the mountain. In the evening when we headed home, the dog bounded up the hill to our chalet and scratched on the front door. He was always invited to join the family for the night. If we were not home, he simply went to one of the other chalets and repeated his scratch on the door routine. As official area mountain dog befriended by all, he never lacked for an invitation. All of the owners living on the mountain were delighted to welcome him for a short visit or a longer sleepover.

Otto had another important job, that of after-school greeter. Our three children often began their school day by using their book bags as improvised skis, sliding on them down from our chalet to the base lodge, before crossing Route 94 to catch the school bus. After school, they walked back from the bus stop across the street and hopped on the #1 chairlift. Once they got off at the mid-station, they waited for some competent skier to give them a ride home to the chalet by hitch hiking on the back of the skier's skis. Once dismounted, they were happily greeted by the ever-welcoming Otto.

Otto did have one rather unsettling trait, however. If a woman arrived at the area with a Stone Martin stole, complete with its furry animal head wrapped around her neck, Otto growled loudly, letting this neck piece creature know that this was Otto's turf, not to be challenged.

Otto also had one curious habit. Beware the unsuspecting if you happened to leave a car window open while visiting the offices across from the base area or chanced to park for the day in the ski school lot. One day, Bill Katterman, ski columnist for the Newark *Star Ledger*, met with us to write a story about Great Gorge. After the interview, Bill went to his car and warmed up the engine. He heard a rustling sound from the back seat. Bill turned to find Otto sitting up, drooling and smiling with a look of "Pleased to meet you Mr. Katterman" on his face.

On another occasion, ski instructor Barry Backer had left the area and was driving up Breakneck Road to his home in Highland Lakes. It was a dark and windy night, the trip up this hill was extremely steep and required lots of concentration. Halfway up Breakneck Road, Barry felt what he thought was a hand on his shoulder. He froze thinking that he was going to be conked on the head and robbed. He glanced around and, to his dismay, found Otto perched on the back seat exhibiting his patented people greeting. Barry turned the vehicle around and sheepishly returned the stowaway to the resort premises. Ever after, however, he loved relating his "Meeting Otto" story to anyone who would listen.

One very cold winter night, Otto decided to sleep outdoors in the snow. He must have had a fever because that afternoon he had felt very warm to the touch. We found him in the morning unmoving and resting peacefully under the pine trees in front of our home. What a sad day for all of us at the mountain. Otto was quietly laid to rest in an unmarked spot beside one of the ski trails bordering the gorge. Let us hope that today he is chasing Jeeps and rainbows on some big cloud in the sky. How happy he made so many people feel every day at Great Gorge.

Kurlander Chalet at Great Gorge
Designed by Sandy Mcilvaine architect who also did the lodge at GG

– CHAPTER 9 –

OPENING DAY

Have You Ever Heard of a Platter Pull?

The facts show, that construction on Great Gorge began March 17, 1965. All our advanced publicity promised that the area would open in December of that year. We had some very bad winters while operating Great Gorge. Our first season was no exception.

Come December, the first few trails were cut, the two new chair lifts were in place and the newly hired operators were trained and ready to get our new area up and running. Our faithful bondholders, waiting to use their newly minted season passes, were beginning to grumble. Sharing their frustration were Luis Schafflinger and his six Austrian instructors recently arrived from Killington and living on site, all set to teach the eager skiers who barraged us for information on the promised opening. What we lacked, however, was that vital ingredient, snow.

The weather was so warm that season that we were unable to make snow until the second week in January. We were desperate to get something open. Finally, Matt Baker managed to make some snow with the jerry-rigged assemblage of old pipes, a snow gun and a generator. His early efforts stretched only to the neighbor's cornfield adjacent to our chalet, where we planned to christen a rudimentary beginners' area. The only way we had to get skiers up to the top of that field was the platter pull lift we had bought as a supplementary conveyance.

What, you may ask, is a platter pull? A platter lift, or pull as it is known in the United States, is a j-bar shaped mechanical lift used for pulling skiers up along the surface of the slope. In Europe, these and similar lifts are also known as Poma lifts, so named for the Poma Corporation that first made them. The idea for the lift was conceived in 1908 by Robert Winterhalder and first set up by him in Germany's Black Forest.

Now you know what a Platter Pull is!

Platter pull lifts consist of an aerial steel rope loop running over a series of wheels, powered by an engine at one end. Hanging from the rope overhead are equally-spaced vertical poles or cables attached to a plastic button or platter that is placed between the skier's legs and pulls the skier uphill. Riding a platter pull is tantamount to taking a metal post, putting it in your crotch and sticking it up your butt. (Of course, you are fully clothed when attempting this maneuver.) You then lean back, grab the moving metal rod gismo and prepare to ski your way up the little hill. A common mistake for first-time riders is attempting to sit on the platter, which immediately sends both platter and rider to the ground. Platter pulls are not as elegant as chair lifts, but they get the job done once the novice rider masters the techniques required. Best of all, we could get one set in place as soon as the Sammis' cornfield was covered with artificial snow.

Everyone was so excited that opening day. A throng of people arrived to savor the slopes of the new ski area in Vernon. Only one slope was open. Actually, only the cornfield was open, but the term "slope" sounds better in a press release. Skiers lined up beside the platter pull, ready for help with transportation up the slope. The slope down was gentle with only a few corn husks peeking out here and there to make it more challenging. The field had an incline of about 30 degrees with a vertical drop that was all of 300 feet.

So many people showed up that first day that some reversed the skiing process. They climbed up the hill to the top, skied down and then sidestepped up to the top again. If the lift line was short, they joined the skiers waiting to get on the platter pull, rode up and joined the throngs heading down. Having climbers willing to forego a platter pull ride at least spread the crowds around a little. Crowded or not, everyone thought they had died and gone to ski heaven.

Of course, Jack, John, Al and Matt were all out there on the snow encouraging people and explaining to them how great the whole place would be when we had more snow. We do not have any records of how many skiers bought lift tickets, where they were sold that day or even how much a lift ticket cost. What we do know, is that everyone seemed to be having a good time. To make the occasion more appealing, we offered food cooked on a large barbecue grill and, throughout the day, served hot dogs and hamburgers to all takers.

Once darkness fell and we cleared the last skier from the slope, all of us, kids included, headed over to the Kurlander chalet. We cracked open the Champagne bottles and congratulated each other. You would think we had just completed the Lincoln Tunnel. To us, it felt as if we had built something equivalent to that project.

Winter in 1966 finally arrived at the end of January. Matt went into high gear to get the real snowmaking going and the chairlifts approved for safe operation. We were on our way. The four families continued to pool their resources. Whoever heard of a business plan? We stumbled along with enthusiasm, tackling on a day-to-day basis the insurmountable amount of work yet to be completed.

As things began to settle down that winter into more regular routines, life got even better. Our business plan evolved with a bit more black to be counted at the end of each week. We also enjoyed the unexpected treat of having a distinctive international flavor added to our days. With Luis and his Austrians to teach us, we made impressive strides with our skiing techniques. Off the slopes, Luis was a stickler about the coffee we drank. He insisted on ceramic cups, assuring us that MacDonald's-type paper ruined the flavor. We soon also began to copy him by adding fondue and steak tartar to our diets. Even more fun, was trying to learn to yodel. Most of us mastered the rudimentary technique, but we could never sound as good as those Austrians. Luis and the others had moved into the little house at the back of the Great Gorge parking lot. At Christmastime, they surprised us with their tradition of lighting real candles to decorate their holiday tree. Luis kept the boys under his watchful eye. Still, they managed to make some very good après-ski friendships. Once they began sharing their happy lifestyle with us, everyone's spirits lifted.

The First Real Day of Skiing at Great Gorge

When beginning to research our early days, I asked Matt Baker, head of our Engineering Department and the only original partner still alive, to refresh my memory of our earliest days. His memories vary a bit from mine. What follows is his answer to my query of what was happening in the fall of 1965 as we prepared to open.

"We actually bought the two of them (platter pulls) from Boris Vilhar. We first set one up in the base area for a skiing demo on horrible ski mats. The mats were produced by the Sussex Brush Company. They were zigzag brushes with metal backing. Jack had set up a demo day with Howard Head and Stein Eriksen for publicity purposes before the ski area was open. *(Remember the scene that late October day. Mud everywhere. Ugh.)*

Nordic skier and famous jumper, Art Tokl works out on the mats at GG

Stein arrived early that morning. He parked his Jag near the lodge. When Stein opened the trunk to get a clean white turtleneck, Jack noticed a tennis racket and asked Stein if he wanted to get some exercise. Stein mentioned that he didn't enjoy playing with amateurs. After betting Stein a new pair of ski boots, Jack took him up to the Highland Lakes Country Club and beat him six-love, six-love. Don't know if Jack ever received the boots.

We had set out plywood panels so spectators could walk to the bottom of the artificial ski slope. Stein went up the platter pull. First turn down, he caught an edge in the mats and fell. After a series of curses, he got up and put on a perfect ski demo. What a showman. After the demo that fall afternoon, we all went up to our chalet for a party. People danced so hard that the light fixtures fell off the ceiling downstairs.

I remember opening day differently (from your scene in the Sammis cornfield). As I recall, we had only chairlift #2. Chairlift #2 was the short one in front of your chalet. What a crowd! There were more than enough bondholders to fill the lift line. After about an hour, the brakes failed and the lift reversed. Then the backstop mechanism failed. Luckily, the broken parts of the backstop jammed into the bull wheel and stopped the lift. As we were clearing the lift to fix it, skiers were fighting to get on.

When we reopened two or three weeks later after a thaw, the platter pull came into play as you described. The lift's demise came later when a skier, while exiting at the top, threw the platter into the operator's shack window. The lift pulled the shack over and derailed. The second platter pull was sold to one of the "German Bund" who lived in Mendham."

(Author's note: The other platter pull lift mentioned in the story was sold to Robert Gerber. He installed the lift on his hillside property in Mendham where he and his family enjoyed many years of skiing in their back yard. Members of the Gerber family were also frequent visitors to Great Gorge. On special occasions, Bob sometimes took over our rathskeller bar room and invited us to join him as he served up his wonderful fondue. He was not a member of the "German Bund." He was born and raised in Switzerland, immigrated to the United States, and has run a very successful dry cleaning establishment in Livingston, New Jersey.)

Opening day stories would not be complete without adding the most colorful of stories about Matt Baker and his method for determining whether the temperatures were right for making snow. As related to us by an employee in the Morris County Sheriff's Office, if the reading on the thermometer outside Matt's stone-walled house did not read low enough to make snow, he would take out his .38 pistol and shoot the offending thermometer off the wall. The mason/sheriff's office employee swore he could always tell what kind of year Great Gorge had by the number of times he was called to repair the building!

Peg, Jamie & Judy on rope tow at Snow Ball

– CHAPTER 10 –

NEW YORK SKI SHOW AND THE SECRET RACE AT PORTILLO

During the years that Jack and I were running Great Gorge, we made sure to schedule our days so that each fall we could take a break to attend the New York Ski Show. This fun and exciting week-long extravaganza was held annually in that city's massive New York Coliseum. Credit for its success belongs to two great guys, Harry Leonard and Jerry Simon, who dreamed up the idea of the show and controlled its operation. This enterprising pair began small in the early 1960's but soon attracted every ski area owner and clothing manufacturer of note. They were masters at tapping into the excitement that builds each fall as skiers start thinking of the new ski season soon to come.

Skiers, and everyone associated with the ski business, poured into the Coliseum in early October just to see and be seen. The event was widely regarded as too important to miss. It was there we were introduced to all the newest trends in skiing, everything from the tights and white ski pants of ski fashion to the three-foot skis that were the rage in the 1960's.

A particular highlight each year was to watch Stein Eriksen, the former Olympic medalist from Sweden, demonstrate some fancy turns on an indoor ski slope that moved! Crowds gathered in awe to watch Stein perform. Just imagine this skiing legend executing his precision turns within the limits of a moving slope that was mounted on the raised flatbed of a truck.

The United States Ski Association usually held a large fund raiser in the fall to benefit the United States Ski Team. They wisely scheduled it to run concurrently with the ski show. Most years the fund raiser was labeled a Ski Ball and consisted of dinner and dancing in a swanky New York hotel ballroom. Members of the National Ski Team were on hand as honored guests, which definitely added authenticity to the ball. The ski show gave us all sorts of new ideas for improving our business. The ski balls generated another kind of spark. The glamour of those evenings, no doubt, fueled dreams of someday having one of our own children make the team.

One year in the late 1960's, Harry and Jerry decided to hold the ski team fundraiser at Alice Tully Hall at Lincoln Center. The big draw was having the well-known musical trio, Peter, Paul and Mary, perform live. Proceeds from the event were to support the US Ski Team. For added interest, the first half of the program featured the showing of a feature film entitled *The Secret Race at Portillo*. The film is about a famous FIS downhill race held in Argentina in August, 1966. The race was the first and only World Cup event ever held in South America. All the existing national ski teams of the world competed. *The Secret Race* was so named, we think, because so few spectators could get to this remote corner of the world. The only guests booked at the resort's one hotel were World Cup competitors and officials. Its distance from major airports was too far and too expensive a trip, so few from the press even covered the event.

The film, *The Secret Race*, has grown in popularity in recent years. It has achieved worldwide cult status among ski clubs and skiing fans. Back then, however, the film, like the race, was mostly just a secret. The year of this particular fundraising program, Jack and I arrived at Lincoln Center and easily found a seat in the fifth row. Most of the people around us were ski writers or representatives from the ski industry.

We settled in our seats anticipating seeing this movie. While waiting, we were introduced to two of our top ski team members, Jimmy Heuga and Billie Kidd. Heuga and Kidd had recently medaled in the 1964 Winter Olympic Games held in Innsbruck. They stopped by for a chat and readily signed our programs. Our evening, which had barely begun, was already a success just by meeting these very personable ambassadors for the team. Alice Tully Hall holds about 4,000 people. We were shocked once we started looking around toward the rear of the hall and found it to be empty. The only spectators were sitting where we were, in the first five rows of the gigantic hall. What an embarrassment for Harry and Jerry. Maybe the movie was not going to be a draw, but the two impresarios had booked one of the top singing groups in the United States. Whether this group was being paid a fee or was performing pro bono for the fundraiser, the end result was bound to be embarrassing.

About then, the lights dimmed and the movie began. As we watched, we could sense rustling in the seats behind us. We shrugged and continued to enjoy the film. When the film ended, the lights went up and we were amazed to see that all the seats in the theater were occupied. How could this have happened?

Rumor has it that Harry and Jerry headed out to Broadway and ran around offering free tickets to anyone who would walk over to Lincoln Center to hear this fabulous group of singers. Their music, played now to a packed audience, brought down the house. The evening ended with everyone applauding and whistling.

To this day, I wonder if Peter, Paul and Mary were ever told about the full house at the Alice Tully Hall Lincoln Center. I wonder, too, if anyone, other than Jack and I, caught on to what has to be one of the greatest promotional bits of Yankee ingenuity that ever took place in the Big Apple in the 1960's. Even today, I think of this story whenever I go to Lincoln Center to hear an opera or a concert.

The movie shown at Alice Tully Hall that evening also inspired another notable event. In 1970, Luis Schafflinger had the skiers from our Junior Racing Program compete in the first-ever downhill race at Great Gorge. We called it "The Secret Race at McAfee". Our race started at 6:30am and ran from the top of the mountain to the base area. The start of the race was unusually early because we had to finish the race before the time the ski lifts officially opened at 9:00am.

The race course dropped down from the top of the Jumping Jack trail to Baker's Field. From there, the racers headed on down Cloud 9 which in turn sped them past cheering onlookers standing alongside the Fitzgerald and Kurlander chalets. From there, they rounded the final turn and hurtled downward to the base area's finish line. What an exciting experience for our young racers. They must have felt just like they were competing in the Olympics. Unfortunately for New Jersey skiing history, "The Secret Race at McAfee" was never held again. If anyone has the results from this race, please contact the author. The winner deserves their fifteen minutes of fame.

This article was found in the October 1965 Eastern *SKI NEWS* in their pre-season issue...

AVALANCHE IN PORTILLO . . . Everyone Thought Dead

Shortly after 6:00am, August 11, at the height of the Chilean ski season, eleven members of the Portillo ski patrol were asleep in their concrete hut, close to the hotel. Seconds later, five were dead, killed by a freak avalanche in the supposedly avalanche-free resort.

Thousand of tons of snow and rock, loosened by a week of storms that had dumped up to five feet of snow a day in the Andes, broke free, descending like the hammer of Hell on this playboy resort of western skiing.

The hut in which the patrol was sleeping, a reinforced concrete building that preceded the hotel, was ripped from its foundations and hurled 180 feet down the slope. When it finally came to rest, three North Americans and two Chileans were dead: Ronald Hock of Binghamton, New York, Michael Fogel of Quebec, Milton Orliotti of Portland, Oregon, and Jaime Cubizasuirre and Manfred Arnold, both of Santiago.

Another Canadian, Dick Hawkins, of Montreal, was the first to dig out and bring help from the hotel, which he reached three quarters of an hour later, freezing in his underclothes.

Recalling the avalanche, he said, "It was like being under water. When I stopped rolling, I had to push the snow away from my face to find air. I dug out and couldn't find anybody. I thought everyone was dead."

The hotel itself was untouched, but two lift towers built especially for the 1966 World Championships were crumpled by the snows. And the railroad was blocked by 38 separate snow and rock slides, leaving Portillo virtually incommunicado with the outside world.

Meanwhile, in Santiago, hundreds of skiers waited for transportation to the hotel. Among them were the teams of next year's competing nations, scheduled for the pre-World Championship races on August 14.

The Pre-World Championships were obviously cancelled for that year. The World Championships were held somehow or other as scheduled. It was the last time that the World Cup was ever to be seen in South America. Very few people were there to see that *Secret Race of Portillo*. It is well documented in the film that many ski clubs in New Jersey use it as a fundraiser. "The Secret Race at McAfee" was held. There is no film available.

– CHAPTER 11 –

IN THE JUNGLE

*"In the Jungle, the Mighty Jungle, the Lion Sleeps Tonight,
A-Wimoweh, A-Wimoweh"*

This 1939 traditional South African song, which the Walt Disney Studio later used in its popular productions of The Lion King, sung with zest and an African flare, easily could also have been the theme song of our Zoo at Great Gorge. Certainly, hearing the song still conjures up the workable solution we found to our problems of keeping New Jersey skiing afloat during the late 1960s. We needed more summer revenue. Bob Dietch, a Zoo Master who had formerly operated a zoo in Bergen County, New Jersey, needed a new place to showcase his animals. Once more, Jack supplied the inspiration and "can do", and I the detailed follow-through that brought Dietch and his animals to McAfee. Area locals still recall this combination that worked so well for both of us from 1967-1972 when Great Gorge was operating independently and Bob Dietch had an ideal place to run his zoo.

By the winter of 1967, the growth and development that had come to Bergen County prompted the landowner who had previously leased his land to Bob for use as a zoo to cancel that lease in favor of making a fortune developing the land on which it sat. Dietch had been forced to move his animals to a rented barn in Sussex County near Wawayanda State Park.

Jack arranged to meet Bob Dietch at the zoo animals' new Sussex County home. The two men negotiated plans to have Dietch move his animals over to Great Gorge each summer and open up this zoo as a public attraction. In addition to our signature lion, Bob's rather extensive collection included a camel, two giraffes, an aoudad, several monkeys, seals, parrots and other beautiful birds, a baby elephant named Obey, and a playful chimp named Oliver.

As summer approached, the area in front of the base lodge and on over to the Beginner's slope alongside the Kamikaze lift took on a whole new look. Assorted cages and fenced-in areas were set up for onlookers to view a very different kind of recreational player. The transition from winter to summer also went smoothly because Charlie O'Brien and so many of his hard-working crew of Mountain Men snowmakers were happy to stay at work as zookeepers.

Some of our favorite memories of this period of Great Gorge history include two rather unusual events. The animals all appeared to be content and well fed. Perhaps, however, a few were just curious and anxious to explore their newest home.

One quiet evening in the summer of 1971, an aoudad escaped from his digs at the Zoo. An aoudad, for the less-informed animal lover, is a wild North African sheep possessed of long curved horns and a long fringe of hair on his neck and forelegs, a description that matched Bob's animal reasonably well.

As the undocumented story goes, in the dead of night as his unsuspecting keepers dozed, this large horned animal managed an escape. He broke out and headed toward the brook which ran down the mountain at the lower end of the main trails. The speculation goes that the aoudad then jumped into the brook, swam through the storm drain under Route 94 and headed toward the Great Gorge sewerage treatment plant. He managed to get around the sewerage plant and plunged back into the brook that flowed over to Black Creek. From there, he headed north toward the Playboy Hotel construction site. As he, or perhaps she, approached the seven-story building, he was temporarily halted by a deep and fairly large, square concrete area that blocked his path. Unsuspecting, he dashed forward only to find himself trapped at the bottom of the seven-foot deep end of the hotel's future swimming pool. Vernon's finest were summoned to the scene. The local fire department and rescue squad managed to rig a sling, lift the captured animal into a waiting net and transport him safely back to the zoo. Ever after, his zoo enclosure was doubly secured to prevent any repeat performances.

Bob's chimp, Oliver, often went to the George Inn at night with Charlie and some of the other men in his crew. While the men relaxed and were eating their hamburgers, Oliver would seek out the container that held the restaurant's paper napkins. He would then proceed to munch on napkins until he was stuffed. An evening filled with this kind of entertainment usually meant a visit to the local vet to extricate the moisture-sucking napkins out of Oliver's stomach. After several such repeat performances, the crew was forbidden to ever again to take Oliver to either the George Inn or to Gary's Vernon Inn, the two local watering holes of choice where "the elite slink to drink". The local Animal Control, Vernon Board of Health and Humane Society also thanked us for this happy turn of events.

Bob Dietch & Companion

Even during ski seasons, Jack sometimes enjoyed visiting Dietch and his animals in their winter home. The two men passed the time swapping stories and dodging the turds which were hurled at them by the chimps. Jack and Dietch retaliated by picking up the turds and hurling them back at the attacking chimps, fortunately still in their cages. The challenge for all parties was to duck at the right time.

When the Great Gorge Zoo closed in 1972, Bob opened a smaller version somewhere else. The last Jack heard of Dietch was when he read in the Vernon paper of an accident near the farm where Bob kept his animals off-season. When the local rescue squad arrived with the "Jaws of Life," they were astounded to find Dietch and a large lion snuggled up to each other in the rear of the smashed vehicle. They both survived the ordeal.

We have no recent information about Bob. A Google search suggests that he has lived on into his 90's and may have retired to Bradenton, Florida. One hopes his animals also continue to live out their lives, well-fed and peacefully making new friends.

Dietch's best friend!

Al & Jill feed the elephant – Barbara Scott & daughter

GREAT GORGE ZOO

– CHAPTER 12 –

THE BUNNIES ARE COMING

In early 1967, Jack heard rumors that the Playboy Club was looking for an eastern location for a resort-oriented club/hotel complex. Playboy, with Hugh Hefner at the helm, had already exhibited their ability to open clubs across the United States. Now they were looking at the possibility of opening a year-round resort within a 50-mile radius of New York City.

Jack's very dear friend, John Cassidy, had recently purchased a great piece of property on Route 517. It ran from Route 517 across part of the valley to a large piece of roadside frontage just north of our offices on the westerly side of Route 94, opposite the Great Gorge Ski Area. Jack met with John to discuss his property. With only a handshake and some scribbling on a napkin from the Sussex Queen Diner, they worked out their agreement. John and Jack always operated that way. Each trusted the other to do their best to make dreams become a reality. In today's business world, it's hard to imagine two men sitting down and making a pledge to each other that, if possible, they would work together to make their deal successfully come to fruition.

John had originally bought this piece of property because it seemed to be the perfect place for the horses and cattle he enjoyed raising. The animals he was grazing there, in turn, loved the sunny exposures and rich pastures his land offered them. John's property had ample acreage and beautiful undulating terrain with rather extensive wetlands, ideal for dairy farming. Jack saw it otherwise. Plenty of electrical power was available nearby and the natural gas pipeline which crossed the property was buried a safe distance underground. The site's location was a comfortable hour-plus drive time from New York City. He convinced John that perhaps his idyllic country plot of land might be destined for greater things.

With Jack's keen eye, he could look at the property and envision what could be built there. It was perfect for a championship golf course, he speculated. The soil that was present then often was, and continues to be, rather mushy. This makes walking or driving a golf cart in those areas an adventure. The squish, squish steps that the golfer treads as he slogs his way through to the green only makes the game a bit more challenging. You had to play this course like a man! With today's environmental restraints, much of the course Jack envisioned would never have met the exacting standards set by the EPA. Personally, I fail to see how a few people walking, hitting a ball and sometimes driving a small electrically operated cart across this property could be much of an environmental disaster.

Sometimes, too, I think back on the comments Sussex County Attorney Richard Downes made when he was describing Jack's unique abilities. "He was like a Mozart who could hear the music in his head and then transfer that music to a manuscript," said Downes. Like Mozart, what Jack was able to create enriched our lives.

Jack could not hear Mozart's music when he looked at land, but he marched to his own beat when it came to land development. He could envision a property and in his mind see exactly where everything would fit. This time, his picture for John included a 28-hole golf course, a building that could become a 500-600 room luxury hotel and parking lots with leftover acreage that could someday be converted into vacation residences, townhouses and single-family homes.

Of course, the one transformation he never foresaw was what was to become of the old barn that John Cassidy had used to house his animals during long nights and inclement weather. The iconic Bunnies of Playboy fame needed a place to stay. John's large country barn ultimately became the unexpected spot of choice when the Bunnies needed housing. Jack was too busy focusing on planning the golf course he expected to enjoy often during the ensuing years.

Maybe a part of Jack's incredible success in visualizing future golf courses can be attributed to the fact that he was such an excellent golfer. Jack played golf to a 10 handicap in those days. He could sure hit that ball on the sweet spot almost every time. Typically, those balls did not have much altitudinal trajectory but, once they hit the ground, they would roll for another 50-plus yards. How did he do that? " Must be in the wrist release," he would modestly reply.

Jack contacted the Playboy decision makers and set up meetings for them to visit John's property. Arnold Morton, the executive head of development and probably a corporation officer, agreed to come out to look at the property. To smooth the way, we mailed him all the topographic maps, town records, zoning ordinances and miscellaneous information one needed to make a decision before going into contract to purchase the property.

Arnold had requested that several scaffolding-type viewing towers be set up at key spots on the property. From these towers, the viewer could enjoy a 360-degree view of the vistas that swept across the tract from the site proposed for the hotel to the land suggested for a potential golf course. Unfortunately, Arnold had never noticed in his advanced reading of the maps and photos we sent him that the tracks of the Lehigh and Hudson Railroad ran on the easterly side of the property under consideration.

Arnold climbed one of the towers and looked all about. Suddenly, as he looked through his binoculars, Arnold began shaking. His voice rose to a shout. "What the hell is that?" he sputtered. He was visibly trembling. The 2:00pm train was roaring down the valley creating a very loud rumbling sound. The blast from the engineer's whistle on the front of the train soon added to the cacophonic music echoing across the valley.

Jack was certain that the deal was going to fall by the wayside, spoiled by a silly train potentially crossing a future cart path. In all of our planning, no one had ever considered that possibility. We took for granted that two or three trains a day, winding their way through the valley, would not be a deterrent. In Jack's rose-colored view of the world, this would only add character to the course. We were often lulled to sleep by the clickety-clickety-clack we heard on the evenings that the 10:00pm express ran through the valley. We always felt that it sure beat the honking of horns on the New Jersey Turnpike.

Shortly after Arnold left that afternoon, he called to say we had a deal, pending approvals from the various governing agencies that would have to review the project. Jack was elated and quickly shifted into his all-systems-go mode of hyperactivity. While we were waiting for these final approvals, Arnold invited our family to visit the Playboy Club in Lake Geneva, Wisconsin. At that time, the Playboy Club had been operating there for about ten years. After it was sold to Americana it was transformed into the Grand Geneva Resort and Spa.

Our trip was top secret. The kids were sworn to secrecy and warned that they were not to discuss the purpose of the trip with anyone. We packed our bags and set off in the 40-foot Winnebago which, for many years, had been our family's way of touring the country. Each kid was allowed to bring one guest. Imagine the thrill for all six of these young kids to be housed in the Hefner Suite. The suite itself came complete with four televisions, a hot tub and a Jacuzzi.

We left the suite to explore the indoor and outdoor swimming pools and the multiple hiking and biking trails that encircled the whole resort. Back inside, we feasted on rich varieties of tantalizing gourmet food. Throughout the resort, no guest could miss the ever-present, voluptuous Bunnies waiting to take our orders for drinks or food. What a far cry from life in downtown McAfee. After several days of such unaccustomed luxury, we headed back to Great Gorge so that Jack could let his partners know that the deal was a go.

During our visit, Jack's admiring eye was caught by the snappy courtesy cars made available for use by VIP's staying at the resort. The Club kept a small fleet of Shelby Cobra GT 500's for these special guests. One particular model was a convertible painted a flashy blue with an offset racing stripe that ran from the front of the car to its rear and over the spoiler which rose majestically in the back. The spoiler, we guessed, was to keep the car on the ground when accelerating rapidly.

Shortly after we arrived home, the convertible, or its identical twin, was delivered to our door at the chalet. This was hardly the vehicle in which I pictured myself driving the kids to school, baseball games or ski races. My driving experience had been acquired by handling a beat up Chrysler station wagon. I tried driving the fancy new upgrade a few times, but I tended to panic every time I had to stop at a red light. Sometimes, to my left on a wider four-lane road, I would hear the challenging vroom, vroom from an 18 year-old male, ready to race me roaring down Route 23. I suspected I could have beaten him, hands down, with my Shelby. I declined all challenges, however, content to proceed at my legal speed limit down to what was then the nearest A&P in Kinnelon.

A few weeks later, we put an ad in the county newspaper. An excited young man promptly purchased the car and happily drove it away. We speculated that we would soon be hearing that he had smashed the beautiful fiberglass convertible, demolishing it. After driving the car for about a month, he managed to do just that. If I had been smart, I would have put the car in a barn nearby, left it there for 30 years and then sold it for the price of a suitable retirement nest egg. That would have been too simple. The actual happening makes for good story telling and reminds me years later, that "The best things in life are free". Looking back, going with Plan B would have been nice, but then I would have one less retirement story and no Shelby story to share with you today.

Several years later, the Playboy Club at Great Gorge in beautiful downtown McAfee became a reality. The Club opened officially in December of 1971. It surely was the biggest thing to ever hit Sussex County and the surrounding areas.

Opening night was scheduled to coincide with the Christmas holidays. The hotel was filled. Skiers came out in droves. Opening weekend featured the actress, singer-dancer, Ann Margaret displaying her wonderful talent. Waitresses with their tight-fitting bunny outfits and their signature large bunny-ears and fluffy tails also attracted spellbound onlookers. On opening night, a huge din-

---

THE RESORT THAT JACK BUILT

The resort is Great Gorge and the man is Jack Kurlander, a self-made man in the American dream tradition.

BY JEFF GARLICK

The honorary president of Great Gorge ski area is a St. Bernard named Otto. Well, not really. That is, he's not really a St. Bernard. But then is Great Gorge really a ski area? Or for that matter, is Great Gorge really real?

About six years ago, when Otto was the lone resident of a stretch of land along route 94 in McAfee, New Jersey, Jack Kurlander and John Fitzgerald scraped together $30,000 each to turn the land into a ski area. Today the area is worth $6,500,000, and Otto follows Kurlander everywhere.

To finance expansion, Great Gorge has sold two bond issues to skiers. The first was a $1,000 series and raised $260,000 while the second netted about $700,000 in $3,500 units. The issues were attractive because of the dividend options—straight 3 per cent interest, or 3 per cent interest and a season pass, or no interest and a season pass with preferred liftline privileges. Needless to say, skiers naturally choose the last two options, so servicing over $1,000,000 in debt costs Great Gorge a paltry $9,000 annually. And the bonds have appreciated to the point where bonds from the original $1,000 series are selling for around $1,400 each. Kurlander says there is a hidden benefit, too: The bond buyers turn out to be the area's best salesmen. After all, they have an interest in it.

The latest expansion program, Great Gorge North, is connected to the original Great Gorge by trails and lifts and was opened in mid-December, completely lit, covered entirely with man-made snow and served by three Borvig double chairlifts.

At the same time, Playboy opened its splendiferous $20,000,000 hotel extravaganza about a mile away across the valley. Playboy is offering 700 rooms in two eight-story wings spreading out from a three-level main lodge. In the lodge area are nine different entertainment and dining rooms, a 24-hour-a-day delicatessen, sidewalk cafe and extensive meeting and banquet facilities.

There is also an exhibit hall with a capacity for 2,220 people or 180 display booths. And the recreational facilities are endless: Right now, there are 27 golf holes. A skeet range, fishing ponds, horseback riding facilities, indoor and outdoor tennis courts, indoor and outdoor pools, a cross-country skiing area, a snowmobile track and a skating rink are on the way. The Playboy complex also has an assortment of health clubs plus a shopping arcade where Great Gorge has a sporting goods store.

Next winter, a Jigback tram will connect Playboy and Great Gorge, landing skiers in the new Great Gorge North area, but for this season it's strictly buswise.

Last winter, Kurlander says the entertainment (he insists he's not in the ski business) at Great Gorge logged 250,000 skiers, running 14 hours a day nonstop seven days a week. This year, with lift capacity increased to 12,000-an-hour from 7,000, and parking facilities expanded by 160 spaces, Kurlander expects 350,000 to 400,000 skiers. And if past performance is any indication he will hit it.

Kurlander's area management creed is simple. You must have night skiing, you must have snowmaking and you must be in business in the summer. Well, anyway, it sounds simple.

For night skiing, the Gorge is only 90 minutes from downtown Manhattan, about 52 driving miles. When you're there at night, it's difficult to tell, either by the visibility or the number of people, whether it's night or day. And Great Gorge people are avid skiers. Last winter, I was leaving the area around 6 p.m. It was drizzling steadily. A car roared into the slot beside mine and a breathless skier leaped out. "How's the skiing?" he asked. "Well, uh, you know it is raining," I said. "I didn't ask that," he replied. "I asked 'how's the skiing?'"

Kurlander's snowmaking operation, powered by a 3,000-horsepower jet engine he got in a deal with Curtiss-Wright covers every inch of ski terrain on the moun-

Builder Kurlander claims he's in the entertainment, not the ski business

Playboy ski bunnies are all part of the fun at the Gorge.

120

SKI FEBRUARY 1972

ner party was planned in the ballroom. All of us – Jack, Peg, John, Anna, Matt, Millie, Al and Ellie-- were the guests of Hugh Hefner. He stopped by our table several times to shake hands and offer thanks. We were so proud of our accomplishment. We had been the catalysts for what promised to be one of the finest resorts ever built on the east coast. The evening was a blast for each one of us and we popped a number of bottles of champagne to celebrate our efforts.

Over the years, top entertainers continued to visit the resort and supply us with lots of great music and comedy. Among the more famous visitors were Sammy Davis Jr., Johnny Cash, The Monkees, Franki Valli and Don Rickles. Our favorite comedian was Bill Cosby. He loved coming to McAfee to perform. What many people do not know about Cosby's visits was that he also loved to play tennis with Jack's brother, Bob. At the time, Bob Kurlander was the resident tennis pro at the Playboy Club and he loved a good game whenever one was to be found. Whenever Cosby was booked at the club, it was a very welcomed event. Jack and, occasionally, future Vernon Valley owner Gene Mulvihill joined in for some fabulous doubles.

One spring day, Gene Mulvihill and Jack were playing tennis as part of a charity event in the Trenton area. The tennis segment of the program was held nearby at Princeton's tennis facilities. Jack and Gene were warming up on court five. Cosby was assigned to the number one show court. Bill looked down the length of courts and with a wave to Jack shouted enthusiastically, "Hey there Lefty! How 'ya doing?!" The very sophisticated group assembled there watched with amusement as this rather unorthodox exchange of greetings echoed through the hallowed halls of Princeton University.

Naturally the new hotel complex triggered many changes in Vernon Township. The greatest economic benefit was the creation of so many of the new service jobs that were needed to make the resort run smoothly. Along with new jobs came new workers, who in turn, needed new housing and their children new schools. Vernon blossomed as a newly minted "Boom Town". Other long-term effects were less obvious. One rather surprising example was the need created in the neighboring towns for the purchase of additional fire engines in case the new six-story building or all the new housing developments were threatened by fire.

We in the ski business had predicted that the arrival of so many hotel guests would in turn lead to selling additional ski lift tickets needed to cover the costs of running the mountain profitably. With this rosy future in mind, Jack had expanded his dream for the Great Gorge Ski Area to be doubled in skiable area. Once approvals were obtained and the Playboy Club was headed to Vernon, Jack began planning and building the all-new Great Gorge North. The expanded ski area opened to great fan fare in February 1972, two months after Hefner and crew had brought their Bunnies to our valley.

At first, there was a large increase in business. The new facility at North was challenging and featured a double chairlift for the ride to the top of the mountain. Once there, the views of the hotel and surrounding areas were, and are today, absolutely breathtaking. Hamburg Mountain is beautiful in all seasons. Whether snow-covered in the winter months (we hoped!), boasting multiple shades of green in the spring and summer, or becoming a photographers' paradise when fall colors are in full bloom, our mountain rivals the best.

The year-round attraction of this overwhelming natural beauty continued to draw more visitors to our valley, and ever more numerous skiers filled our slopes in the winter months. Little did we suspect, however, the sharp turns that lay ahead.

Great Gorge North –
Opening Ribbon Cutting

Mayor Ed Snooke
Head of Economic Development –
Jules Marron –
Assemblyman Bob Littell
John
Matt
Jack
Al

– CHAPTER 13 –

RACING, JUMPING, SLIDING, BUMPING

Like other changes in our Twentieth Century American lifestyle, skiing and the industry that grew up to service it also changed drastically. Early on only royals and wealthy Americans able to travel to the playgrounds of the Swiss Alps found skiing affordable. From mid-century onwards, however, Americans of all social strata began to take up skiing in ever growing numbers. By century's end, skiing had become the winter sport of choice. We, in turn, were fortunate to catch the start of skiing's earliest popularity and to have ridden along with its cresting popularity.

Jack loved to tell us of what skiing was like in the early days. During his high school years in the early 1940's, he made frequent ski trips to Mount Marcy in northern New York State. He and his friends loved this great outdoor experience. Ski outings for him, in addition to a few trips down a hill, meant camp fires, snowshoeing, mountain climbing and visiting with the many deer that stopped at their lean-to for a snack. When driving to the North Country from New Jersey, spotting another car with skis mounted on top was a novelty. Once spotted, occupants of both cars would cheer, honk horns and wave enthusiastically. Today, a car roaring along the New York Thruway with skis on top hardly rates a second glance.

Skis in the 1930's and 1940's were wooden maple or hickory boards, seven to eight feet in length. They presented tremendous challenges to their passengers. The skier in his loose-fitting leather laced boots strapped himself tightly to these cumbersome conveyances by means of leather long-thongs. Depending upon snow conditions, the bottoms of these wooden skis had to be hand waxed with paraffin or a similar wax. If the winter weather was warm and the snow softening, the skier had to stop often to re-wax if he wanted to prevent his skis from collecting hunks of snow on the bottom. Today's high-tech bindings and shorter parabolic "shaped" ski with their slick bottoms combine to make the sport easier to master and far safer.

Jack's 1940 Northland-model skis were made of solid hickory and had a bear claw toe-piece to hold his boots. Once the Northland Company began attaching metal edges to their post World War II models, Jack was happy to upgrade. In 1954, Howard Head introduced the first aluminum sandwich skis.

Jack, always the innovator, was one of the first to buy one of those early models. Jumping off trail-side cliffs in the early 1950's was the challenge of choice for the more advanced skiers. Now skiers jump off man-made jumps at the terrain parks most ski areas have added to their slopes. One day, Jack overshot the landing and demolished his old all-aluminum skis, which were made by the Head Ski Company and looked a bit like mom's aluminum pots. They had been widely acclaimed as stronger, better and longer-lasting than any of the wooden ones the miracle metal aluminum had replaced.

Jack sent a regretful letter off to Howard Head, developer and owner of the company. In it, Jack explained that he was an "occasional weekend skier" and asked for a five-foot pair of the new fiberglass-composite style 360 model for his "new bride". Howard answered by saying he would be happy to comply but that, in exchange, he would like to have Jack's bent skis to put in the Howard Head Ski Museum in Baltimore, MD. The deal was done. Presumably, today Howard's heirs still own Jack's old skis, identifiable by the number 24 etched on the top, meaning they were from the first batch of this model. No one knows for sure, however, just where those old skis are today.

Once Great Gorge had broken ground and was attracting pre-opening attention from the ski world, Jack and Howard Head came to know each other better. Howard even came to some of our promotional days. As I recall, Howard was there that October day when Stein Eriksen tore his ski pants while demonstrating a turn on the artificial plastic-brush ski slope we had set up near the base area.

From the beginning, Great Gorge was the host for all sorts of exciting ski competitions. Skiers, young and old, always seemed to love these new challenges. Before we had any organized races, the kids who lived on the mountain and some of their friends invented their own. They built a little trail through the woods next to our house. Afternoons after school they could be seen climbing up and racing down their little trail, carving turns around a set of make-shift poles, and envisioning themselves plunging down some famous Austrian race course. So occupied, they rarely got into any trouble – or any that we know about. Unknowingly, without any outside encouragement, they were busy perusing excellence in ski racing. Hopefully, young snowboarders, who today greatly outnumber skiers at so many ski areas, have the same kind of passion that it takes to achieve excellence in their sport.

As, mentioned earlier, Luis Schafflinger came to us from Badgastein, Austria via Sugarbush, Vermont, to head up our Great Gorge Ski School. The Austrians he brought with him were a very professional group, happy to teach Americans how to clamp their legs together and execute some very classic Austrian turns. The Austrian style was definitely more elegant than the snow-plow and stem-christie turns we neophytes employed. Our early skiers, especially the kids, were very receptive to the new style, and the quality of skiing seen on our slopes improved rapidly. The new style also meant skiers could ski faster and turn more quickly, which in turn led to thoughts of matching skills and competing in head-to-head competitions.

Luis soon suggested organized ski racing as a next step for the kids at the Gorge. He and his son, Manfred, spearheaded the budding racing programs. He started the youngest kids off with weekly lollipop races on the lowest slopes of the mountain. Their older sisters and brothers began working out several times a week following their experienced Austrian models down the mountain or through the gates.

Jack goes for the Gold in Nastar!

Soon the race program picked up serious racers from all over the surrounding New York/New Jersey area. Ultimately, our coaches guided several young skiers on to national and even, in a few instances, to international competitions. Still other products of the Great Gorge Race Team went on to compete on the college level.

Once the parents became involved, they soon encouraged the kids to enter some Eastern Ski Association sponsored competitions. The first race we chose for our area kids to enter was at Belleayre in New York's nearby Catskill Mountains. We knew very little about the requirements, one of which was that racers must wear helmets to compete.

Our young competitors arrived, signed in, and were advised of some of the rules. First and foremost, they were reminded they were required to wear

Ski jumping – new sport at Great Gorge

helmets. We had brought along three helmets. They were going to have to be shared by the ten kids who had made the trip with us. Thinking quickly, we organized The Helmet Brigade. Translated, that meant grab the kid as he crossed the finish line, quickly remove his helmet from his head, start climbing with the helmet back toward the start, pass the helmet on to the next waiting parent, and finally get the helmet secured on the next competitor's head. I can still picture Anna Fitzgerald huffing and puffing as she ran up the hill with a bushy fur hat on her head, topped off by a bulky silver-striped ski helmet clamped on top of her hat. She covered a good distance before passing the helmet on to Jane Pier, who in turn relayed it on to the next parent until it arrived at the top where the next kid was waiting to make his run. This routine continued for a very exhausting two hours.

Then, as now, other parents along on the trip served as gatekeepers. They checked each racer as he passed by to be sure he navigated correctly through the course. Between racers, gatekeepers shoveled snow and did whatever was needed to keep the course safe. Gate keeping, we learned, can be a cold and snowy or rainy activity. Racing parents seldom had any trouble sleeping at night.

Jumping ahead a bit, one more race story needs to be told. When I was General Manager at Hidden Valley, I became tired of not doing very well in the weekly club races that the area held for its members. One day I "commanded" Ski School Director Joe Riggs to hold a special race for me. It was aptly named The Peg Kurlander Chicken Slalom. I told Joe that I would set the course by taking a practice run. I THEN WANTED THE POLES PLACED WHERE I HAD MADE THE TURNS. As I skied down, everywhere I turned, a dutiful patroller planted the poles, marking the gates where other racers were required to turn when they skied down in the course I had set. Several of my most loyal employees agreed that was pretty fair. The disappointed winner never even received a trophy for that event. Unfortunately, since the race was never held again, my Chicken Slalom title could not even be defended.

Peg easily wins Chicken Slalom

About the time that Luis was beginning to build a racing program at the area, Jack learned that the world famous Nordic ski jumper, Art Tokle*, resided in nearby Lake Telemark, NJ. Jack's first thought, quickly put into action, was to encourage Art to consider running a Nordic program at Great Gorge. A full Nordic program includes cross country skiing as well as ski jumping. The snowmaking guns which we already had in place to cover our present trails were operating to capacity. Our water reserves might be strained if we were to cover additional cross country trails. Jack decided he would ask Art to head the program, but to concentrate on ski jumping, Art's known specialty. Tokle was thrilled to be invited and soon joined the staff at Great Gorge.

In summer of 1968, a ski jump was built on the southern most side of the area alongside Route 94. On a trial basis, the jump runway and take off were covered with nylon bristled mats. More mats were put down for the landing and its run off. The area kids went crazy trying out this new adventure. As soon as the fall turned cold, we replaced the matting and covered the jump and the landing area with machine-made snow.

*Arthur Tokle was born in Lokken-Verk, Norway, and came to the US in 1947. He was US Ski Jumping Champion in 1951 and 1953, a member of the 1960 Olympic Team and three World Championship Teams. After his coaching days, Art remained a great friend and supporter of ski jumping, attending many eastern competitions and assisting with coaching and hill preparation. Art was known for always having a good word for every ski jumper, even the most inept. Art's older brother, Torger Tokle, also born in Norway, became one of the greatest US jumpers. Arthur died in 2005, 60 years to the day that his brother Torger was killed in combat in Italy while serving with the US Army's 10th Mountain Division.

Art worked diligently to integrate cross country and ski jumping programs and competitions with the popular alpine skiing already available at Great Gorge. The growing crowds who came to enjoy Great Gorge soon dictated that there was not sufficient space available to run both activates profitably. Cash flow won out over Nordic. The Nordic approach could not survive another season.

Art Tokl brings ski racing coaching skills to GG

The racing program continued to be a big activity at Great Gorge. In 1970, a specially designated racing trail, timing tower and racing chairlift were installed on the southern side of the mountain. Competitors then had their own area on which to train and compete. That chairlift that served the old race trail is still one of the only lifts in the United States that rides above and over another lift. In later years, almost all club, high school and USSA-sanctioned competitions were held at Great Gorge North or were moved over to the Hidden Valley Ski Area.

Jamie Kurlander was one of the earliest success stories of the Great Gorge Racing Program. From her first days in the program, and even though one of the youngest, she improved rapidly. By the age of 14, Jamie became the first person from New Jersey to be selected as a member of the US Ski Team. She competed internationally with the team for nine years then went on to compete with the Women's Professional Ski Association for a number of additional

Jamie Kurlander shows her World Cup technique

years. She and husband, Dean Peters, currently own and operate three ski shops in Park City, Utah. The Kurlander ski legend does not end there. Jamie and Dean's three children – Max, Tosh and Tali – continue to compete in Freestyle Aerial and Mogul events held throughout the United States. Closer to home, Jamie was recently inducted into the Sussex County Sports Hall of Fame.

Donna Weinbrecht from High Crest Lake in West Milford, New Jersey, also began her early racing days at Great Gorge and continued her race training at Hidden Valley. In 1979, when the FIS recognized freestyle as a sport, she switched over to moguls and aerials and moved her training base to Killington, Vermont. Donna was the first American skier to excel in mogul competition. She capped her career by winning the Olympic Gold Medal in the mogul freestyle event during the 1992 Winter Games held in Albertville, France. The win was particularly notable because it marked the first time that Freestyle events were officially medal events at the Winter Olympics. She, too, has recently been voted into the Sussex County Sports Hall of Fame.

Danny Kass, another Sussex County-bred notable, began skiing at Great Gorge and Hidden Valley. At the age of 12, however, he switched his competitive allegiance to snowboarding. He has since been rewarded by winning two Silver Olympic Medals and several X-Games competitions while performing his aerial tricks in the half-pipe events.

The four Pier boys, also original skiers in the Great Gorge program, have continued to be active in the sport. Johnny made All American while racing at Williams College. Today he is a physician living in Freeport, Maine, and often volunteers his time as Team Physician for the US Ski Team during their summer training camps in South America. Jeff Pier raced at St. Lawrence University and for a number of years afterward remained on as their head coach. From there he returned to New Jersey and continued coaching at Hidden Valley. David Pier, who now resides in Rockland, Maine, raced while at Bates College and coached part-time at Sugar Loaf Mountain. Greg Pier, the eldest brother, owns Heino's Ski and Bike Shop in Pompton Plains. Mom and Dad continue to enjoy living slopeside at Hidden Valley.

The racing program continued for many years at Great Gorge, but moved elsewhere after the original owners of Great Gorge left in 1978. Life has also taken its toll on the coaches who ran the program for so many years.

Luis Schafflinger was killed in an avalanche in Badgastein, Austria. His son, Manfred, returned home to Austria where he continues instructing skiers. Rip McManus was killed in a car accident one night on a dark road in Sussex County.

After Luis departed, Dave Scott took over the program and coached at the Gorge for a number of years, ably assisted by Glen Newman. Dave moved on to Colorado and was recently inducted into Colorado's Ski and Snowboard Hall of Fame. Glen followed him there and he, too, continues to instruct young racers.

The last head coach to be appointed to the Great Gorge program, Bruce Crane, also transferred his teaching to the western states. When last heard from, Bruce reported that he was still active in USSA events. Dave Schneider began his race coaching at Great Gorge, but moved over to Hidden Valley once Joe Riggs was hired to head that program.

– CHAPTER 14 –

THE END OF AN ERA
AT GREAT GORGE

In March of 1974, another ski season was ending at Great Gorge, but this one was different. As had become obvious, the dream we lived and the adventures we shared for the past decade were coming to an end. In the mid-1970's several factors combined to create an untenable situation. Warm winters with very little natural snow, rainy weekends, a spike in interest rates to 18% and gas shortages all took their toll on the number of skiers visiting Great Gorge. The added costs from the construction of Great Gorge North and the disappointing number of skiers staying at the Playboy Club added to the financial woes.

Jack, John, Matt, Al and the new investors who had come on board a few years earlier needed to reassess their futures. Great Gorge was awash in a sea of overwhelming debt. Continuing to run Great Gorge South and Great Gorge North was no longer sustainable. The partners met and agreed that, at season's end, they would accept a buyout offer from the remaining Great Gorge investors. They, in turn, sold their interests to Gene Mulvihill's neighboring Vernon Valley, a ski area, an area owned and operated by the Great American Recreation Company. Jack, John, Matt and Al had no alternative but to sell their proportionate share in Great Gorge to the outside investor group. They were each paid $1.00 for the transfer. After the transfer was complete, each of the original partners still owned his own home, his cars, his kids and any and all of his personal possessions.

Although we tried hard to keep everyone's spirits up, having to leave our beautiful mountain and ending the wonderful partnership we enjoyed for the past ten years was very sad indeed. The night the area closed for the season, the partners, staff, ski patrol and many of the loyal bond and season-pass holders congregated on the base lodge balcony. After ten years of blood, sweat and tears, we were all assembled at the bottom of Hamburg Mountain, where it had all begun in 1964, to say our farewells.   Jack, John, Matt and Al, with hearts filled with pride but with memories mingled with sadness, led the group.

This was the era of "streaking". The evening began with an effort at gaiety. Several employees and patrol members made ritual dashes across the base area in the buff, some on skis and others in snowmobiles, flags waving, kisses thrown in a rollicking and festive atmosphere. One of the streakers from the Ski Shop attempted a Nordic ski streak to the lodge. He slipped when he could not stop and became tangled in the snow fencing. What a sight to see! All the watching spectators laughed so hard that we "barely" had time to remember what was really happening. For obvious reasons, the names of those streakers have been withheld. Who could afford the possible law suits that might ensue from that last night celebration?

Just about the time that the anonymous streaker untangled himself, our attention was drawn to some movement farther up the mountain. Unbeknownst to any of the other employees and spectators, Charlie O'Brien secretly led his gang of awesome Mountain Men across Route 94 and over to the horse stable that was then part of the Playboy Hotel complex. There the gang "borrowed" all the horses, complete with saddles and bridles, and quietly made their way back across Route 94. From there, they proceeded to cross Route 94, then up the entrance road at Great Gorge North, and from there they rode along the access road to Great Gorge South. Once assembled at a marshalling point below the mid-station, the newly minted cowboys headed toward the Cloud Nine slope.

Next, the rousing marching music of the well-known "The Bridge over the River Quai" came from the area's speaker system. This riveting sound echoed for a great distance, across the base area and over to the parking lot. As we looked up the Cloud Nine trail, a whole band of "cowboys" appeared from out of the night shadows and majestically proceeded to ride their borrowed mounts down toward the base area. These apparitions soon took shape, skidding to a stop. They lined up in front of the base area facing the lodge. Once stopped, on cue, they tipped their cowboy hats to Jack, John, Matt and Al and then did the same to the rest of the crowd gathered on the balcony. This was a very moving moment. More hugs and lots of fresh tears followed. Camelot was over.

In the ensuing months following that final evening, the new management from Vernon Valley took over and the Great Gorge/Vernon Valley Ski Area was formed. The story of that merger and of the extensive expansion of recreational activity that followed for the next thirty years is dealt with in later chapters. Sadly, after that final evening, the original Great Gorge partners moved on, seeking new careers and new horizons.

John and Anna Fitzgerald headed north and spent the next two winters managing the Snow Valley Ski Area in Manchester, Vermont. Snow Valley was owned by our mutual friend, John Frohling, a prominent lawyer in Newark, New Jersey. One of John Fitzgerald's first improvements to the Vermont area was to oversee the installation of an additional lift. The old Snow Bowl Ski Area in Jefferson, New Jersey, had recently closed and was selling its lifts. Snow Valley was happy to add another chairlift to their Vermont complex, especially with John on hand to supervise its installation. Unfortunately, even with the added capacity of another lift, Snow Valley found it could no longer compete with the bigger and more glamorous neighboring Bromley and Stratton Mountain areas. Like Snow Bowl and so many others before it, the area closed in the mid-1970's. The Fitzgeralds left Vermont and moved to upper New York State. John accepted a position at the Provimi Veal Company. His new company specialized in quality veal feed that helped produce the outstanding veal offered by the best upscale restaurants. While John sold veal feed, Anna sold real estate. Only after the expanding Vernon recreational businesses offered owner/managers an opportunity at Cobblestone Village in 1986, did the couple return to their native New Jersey to lease a shop and start over again. By this time, the Fitzgerald boys were of adult age and had moved on to new endeavors that did not involve the ski world. John died shortly after their return to New Jersey, but Anna continues to live in the chalet they built at Great Gorge and remains active in local affairs.

Matt and Millie Baker and their three children eventually moved to Virginia where they continued to raise horses. The last we heard from them, Matt had been hired as an engineer for another company not involved with the ski industry, and Millie was taking care of a stable full of fine horses. Their kids – Millie, Dorie and Stokey – spent most of their growing up years there on the Virginia farm, far removed from the skiing scene. Stokey continued to ski regularly, mostly in Colorado, and far away from the crowded areas of the east. His sisters ski rarely. Young Millie is an architect and her sister Dorrie is a pediatrician who also owns and operates her own horse farm.

Al and Ellie Stasium moved with their daughter, Jill, to Sparta to enjoy the less stressful lifestyle that Lake Mohawk offers. They spent many happy days golfing and being active members of the Lake Mohawk Country Club before health issues took their toll. Ellie died a number of years ago and Al passed on in October 2010. Jill is an artist, currently living in Greenwich Village in Manhattan.

Jack, on the other hand, as we shall read, was not ready to abandon the dream. He continued to feel it was so much fun owning a ski area that he should give it another try. As always, he could only see the positive side of any and all situations. I was not as sure that our futures lay in skiing. As always, however, I was ready to stand by my man.

Judy Kurlander

– CHAPTER 15 –

HIDDEN VALLEY

Dream to Reality

After Great American Recreation took over Great Gorge, Jack found he was not willing to give up being part of skiing in Sussex County. He decided the time was right to open a private ski area in New Jersey where members would purchase a yearly membership at an area which was private on weekends and holidays. The advantages of a private club would include no more crowded slopes or tedious lift lines for its members.

As always, Jack could only see the positive side of starting a private ski area. I was not sure about going back into a weather-related business with a high degree of risk. Running a shoe store sounded good to me. Shoes wear out and kids need new ones all the time. In spite of my misgivings about going back into the ski business, I told Jack I would be supportive of his future plans.

Fortunately, this time around, our kids were grown and on their own. Jamie finished Pope John High School and was training year-round as a downhill racer with the United States Ski Team. For financial reasons, John left his college in Boulder, Colorado. He returned home and began to work with Jack, helping him launch another ski area. Judy moved to Telluride to experience the Colorado lifestyle. She found a job as a tour guide, driving the horse drawn sleds down Telluride's Main Street. When not working, she was tearing up the ski slopes at Telluride.

Jack knew Dave Curtis from his work on the ski patrol at Great Gorge. His parents, George and Bertha Curtis, lived in Highland Lakes and owned a large tract of mountain land in nearby Vernon. This property bordered Breakneck Road and could only be reached by driving up Breakneck's very steep grade.

Undaunted by the access, Jack decided this was it! He began by studying the topographic maps and laid out his vision of a smaller, but still challenging complex. He plotted where the best locations for the lodge, parking lots and trails should be. He liked what he saw.

In addition to the ski trails and base area, he envisioned developing land on the top half of the mountain which he named Upper Plateau. It had some excellent land for building homes and ample room to build a large lake which would serve as the water supply for snowmaking and a place for summer activities. He also planned some tennis courts, a swimming pool, ball fields and a small clubhouse. In order to get to the Upper Plateau, he proposed a road from the base area to the top of the mountain. We often referred to it as Break-Your-Neck Road. Today's residents at Hidden Valley have built beautiful homes ranging from chalets to Frank Lloyd Wright contemporary-style houses with spectacular views of Vernon's picturesque valleys. By necessity, most of them ride about in four-wheel drive cars suitable for this rugged terrain.

When satisfied that this was the place to create his next masterpiece, Jack assembled a small group of investors and began negotiating the purchase of the land from George and Bertha. A short time later we moved into high gear and finalized the purchase of Hidden Valley.

The property had its own unique bit of history from the days when Hermit Alex farmed the land and lived there in supreme isolation, beholden only to nature. An article written in 1977 for the fall edition of the Hidden Valley newspaper gives a picture of the remote early days when the Curtis family first arrived in the area. It also sheds a bit more light on why Jack was sure the Curtis property would be a good fit for his ski club.

George and Bertha Curtis of Highland Lakes bought acreage (on Breakneck Road) from Hermit Alex in the 1960's. They envisioned a community of their friends who would live on the land and maintain the natural beauty of the area. Hermit Alex, they promised, could stay on his farm in the hidden valley, reached only by climbing a dirt track. During his lifetime, Alex grew his own food, kept some livestock and only went down into town every month or two for supplies. One bitter winter, the townspeople realized that no one had seen Alex for quite some time. In growing alarm, they hiked the mountainous terrain to find his secluded valley and, sure enough, found that his heart had stopped as he sat on his porch facing the sunset.

The passing of time changed George and Bertha Curtis' plans, and they decided against establishing their own community. Permanent life-time members of the Hidden Valley Club, they are happy to see their land put to recreational use by people intent on preserving the loveliness of the landscape. The name, Hidden Valley of Friendship, which they originally chose just after their purchase, was the obvious choice to adapt for the new ski area.

The road recently built to the upper valley and the site of the present-day tennis courts, where Hermit Alex once had his farm, has been named Curtis Drive.*

---

*Shortly after we purchased the Curtis property, George and Bertha retired to Sarasota, Florida, but returned to visit whenever they were in New Jersey. Sadly, I have learned that they recently passed away, leaving only their namesake, Curtis Drive, to remind us of the fulfillment of the family's early plans for their land.

As soon as the purchase of the Curtis property was finalized, we purchased a small green house located next to what is now the main parking area. Like our early days at Great Gorge, this farm house became our project headquarters for the engineers, surveyors and bulldozer operator. It was also the site of our temporary sales office.

Jack oversaw the work of constructing the ski trails, lifts, base lodge and maintenance building. Once trails were cut, he could start planning where to install the needed electricity, water and snowmaking pipes that turn a mountain into a ski area.

At the same time, he hired architects Jack Murphy and Warren Bendixen to design the lodge. We knew both men from our days at Lake Valhalla in Montville. Their design proved to be as charming as it was functional. It featured lots of beams, chandeliers and Tyrolean trimmings. Several of its decks and balconies overlooked the base area and encouraged moms and dads to watch and wave to their kids whenever they skied past. Inside, design efforts concentrated on making the lodge a unique and welcoming place to buy food and beverages, or to sign up for ski school or equipment rentals.

Particular care was taken to design a place that would make members feel that this was their special clubhouse. One of the many nice touches planned was a members' only private locker room. Members came to love the convenience of storing their skis and boots at the mountain.

Jack was aware that the Snow Bowl Ski Area in Newfoundland, New Jersey, had recently closed. The newer facilities being constructed in Vernon had become too much competition for the small Jefferson Township ski area. Before our Great Gorge days, we all had enjoyed skiing there. It was a lovely family place where we took our own kids to learn to ski.

Jack met with the owners at Snow Bowl and immediately purchased everything in sight that could be moved. Happily for us, we were able to purchase the double chairlift, the rope tow, the snow-making guns, grooming equipment, and much of its cafeteria and kitchen equipment. Along with the big-ticket items, we also were able to buy all the tools and mountain equipment no longer needed by the shuttered, closed ski area.

While we were at Snow Bowl arranging to pick up our purchases, our friend, Amos Phillips, and some of his kids visited us there. We invited them to take any or all the napkins and dried goods left over from the vacant cafeteria. They took so many napkins, I dare say, that they will never have to buy a napkin for home use during their lifetime.

The Borvig Corporation in Pine Island, New York was low bidder on the high-speed triple chairlift we installed at Hidden Valley. The old lift from Snow Bowl was moved to the Chicken Delight beginners trail to service our novice area.

As soon as construction was underway, we began to assemble our management team. Joerg Speck from Vernon came on board as an investor and to handle the job of overseeing mountain construction. In addition to his excellent work outdoors, Joerg proved equally valuable once he came indoors. His earlier experience working at the Walpack Inn helped him oversee the installation of the second-hand kitchen equipment purchased from Snow Bowl. Joerg also was a trained chef, an asset that helped once he took over supervising of the kitchen staff.

Joe Riggs signed on as Ski School Director, and Bob Polhemus took charge of snowmaking and grooming. Both key men had previously worked with us at Great Gorge for a number of years. Jack was General Manager, and I served as his assistant in addition to running the marketing and public relations department. Our son, John Kurlander, tackled group sales. Dave Curtis headed ski patrol.

Betty Hansen was in charge of the kitchen. Although not considered management, Betty was another quality employee and one of Jack's favorites. He was always so proud of our food service and the high standards achieved by Betty. Her homemade soups, biscuits, and pastries were particularly outstanding.

A number of other ski patrollers from Great Gorge joined our staff, including Peter Kalafut and Dennis Fielding. They took jobs working on the

Hidden Valley Ski School Director – Joe Riggs

mountain and digging out the beach area at Upper Plateau. They jumped into the project and did an outstanding job. Dennis is now a physician with offices in Hamburg, and Peter has his own drafting and design company in Franklin. Helen Halum was hired to be Jack's secretary. She did all the organizational work for the offices, scheduling, member record-keeping and the various other tasks that help an organization run smoothly. Miraculously, we were ready for our first season by mid-December 1975.

From the start, both management and support staff functioned very well. Everyone strived for excellence in their specific responsibility, yet blended harmoniously as a team. As soon as our headquarters in the little green farmhouse was operational, we set to work selling memberships in this exclusive, new private ski area.

Visuals worked wonders. Hoping to impress prospective members, we began by running daily Jeep tours to the top of the mountain. The view alone was often our most effective enticement. We worked even harder on special promotions – scheduling pig roasts, barbeques, fish fries and a host of other attractions to convince prospects of the social benefits of membership.

Before the area opened, and once the initial membership efforts began to lag, we started on our plan to offer single-family home sites as a means to raise the funds needed to build the ski area. The response was very positive. With this newest infusion of capital, our ski area construction moved along well. Work also began on the access road to the Upper Valley Plateau where these homes were to be sited. The year was 1974, a full year before we had the area ready to open to skiers.

In my story one incident stands out as a rather mysterious footnote to our early sales efforts and explains a bit about the teamwork that went on behind the scenes. Everyone pitched in wherever needed. Jim Kittel, a CPA and early investor, worked for us part-time helping set up the administrative offices and the accounting department.

Early one morning, Jim was in the office and answered the phone. The caller indicated that he wanted to come to Hidden Valley that day to purchase a membership. Jim said he would be happy to meet him and would give him a tour of the mountain. Several hours later, a red Ford convertible pulled in, with rock music playing loudly on the car radio. The prospect and two very attractive young ladies, who hopped out of the back seat, headed to the green farmhouse office complex. They must have been a bit underwhelmed at the site of our rudimentary welcoming area, which at that time had parking spots for all of about eight cars.

Jim answered all their questions. The "New Member" wrote a check to pay for his first season's membership and then left, waving an enthusiastic goodbye.

A few of our other investors stopped by that morning and asked how things were going. Jim told them about how he had signed up, what was at the time, the first membership to be sold to join the Hidden Valley Club. They were very pleased to hear that news.

Then an excited investor asked for particulars of the sale. Who was he, where did he come from and how had he heard about our wonderful new project? As Jim began to fill in the blanks and describe his easy sale, one of the investors began to chastise Jim. He was sure Jim should not have accepted this membership, since the new member turned out to be a "man of color." To his biased eyes, people would not join Hidden Valley once they heard who wrote the first check. Everyone else thought his membership was a great idea.

The name of the complaining investor is not available for comment. The interesting part of this story is that the check cleared the bank but the mystery man and his friends never returned to Hidden Valley. The mystery continues today with no logical answer to the question of who he was and why he never showed up again.

Even after we opened to the public that first year, membership sales for the private club ski area were slow. Ours was a new concept. The cost of a membership was realistic, but lots of salesmanship and Yankee ingenuity were needed to convince skiers that this was an option worth exploring. In hopes of sparking more interest, we next tested out a one-day trial pass.

When a customer came to the ticket counter, the pitch we made was for him or her to try a day of skiing, without obligation to take out a membership. We sold prospective members a one-day ski pass at a price which was equivalent to what members would pay when they brought a guest. It worked. Even if the potential member did not join, we had the advantage of having the extra revenue from their one-day trial. This was a welcome change. Also, once people did join, they often brought friends and relatives as guests, many of whom then decided to join the club.

Early on, the Weinbrechts from the High Crest Lake section of West Milford, joined as a family and attracted some twenty other families* from the High Crest Lake area to join them. This group of twenty families became one of the lynch pins of Hidden Valley's ultimate success and were our biggest ambassadors for private ski area membership. High Crest members skied often and enjoyed good family fun. Their kids began with the learn-to-ski programs or the toddlers' ski programs, but quickly moved on to the racing programs. Today, we hear that many of the grandchildren of that original group of members continue to ski at Hidden Valley.

---

*Two members of the original group, Dianne Warll and Betsy Wright, continue to be among the author's longest standing and dearest friends. Julie Ann Warll attended Stratton Mountain Ski Academy and continues with Adult Ski Programs at Park City, Utah. Donna Weinbrecht went on to win the first ever Gold Medal awarded in Freestyle Skiing at the 1994 Winter Olympics in Albertville, France.

Jimmy Weinbrecht, ever an innovative leader, set up and started running a freestyle ski program for his kids and any others who were interested. Members' kids were fascinated by this new type of ski competition. Freestyle skiing featured such acrobatics as helicopters, 360's, spreads, twisters, twister spreads and jumps. This competition has evolved. Now we see front flips, back flips, 720's and 1080's, grabs and off-axis jumps.

Once the ski area had successfully opened in the winter of 1975-1976, we could turn our efforts to the top of that road. Ultimately, this part of Hidden Valley became a summer delight. We opened swim and tennis facilities and added access to the lake. We also built a paddle tennis court next to the base lodge. This provided more sports activity between seasons. Next, in addition to the twenty residential homes on Curtis Drive, we added a forty-unit condominium community to the upper plateau area. These new member/investors loved the magnificent, expansive views of the Sussex County countryside. Potential members responded well to this newest opportunity to purchase vacation housing with year-round recreation.

Jack Pays a Price

Beginning again with the launch of a private ski area which would compete with the established Vernon Valley/Great Gorge was stressful. The 1975-1976 diary Jack kept was found in Jack's desk and tells part of the story. His entries, transcribed and reproduced below, were always done in haste, generally at the end of each day or next morning, and hint at the stress he dealt with daily.

The wonder is, that throughout this period Jack, may have noted his worries in his diary, but with us he kept his good cheer. He never brought problems home. If we wondered whether we had done the right thing starting another ski area when we had not made a nickel after 10 years of operating Great Gorge, he never seemed to agree. In spite of the problems he mentions here, Jack remained undaunted. He was always encouraging the men who were out on the mountain making snow and repairing equipment. He treated these mountain men with respect, urged them on, and was quick to show his appreciation for their efforts.

During our first winter of operation, the learning curve for all of us was straight up. If Jack was feeling some of this stress, he never let on, preferring instead to act the cheerleader while telling only the diary some of what really worried him. Jack's primary physician, Lucien Fletcher, often tried to warn him of what was all too easy to ignore. As Dr. Fletcher would admonish to rather deaf ears, "You are in great health, Jack. But what will get you in the end is stress." Here is how Jack chose to see it:

December 22:
Today was one of all problems. The first thing to happen was freezing of the #1 line at the top for approximately 250 feet. The top line split, which required approximately 10 feet of welding. Then, as we were trying to get the ice out of the #1 line, we created too much pressure on the #2 aluminum lines, which then blew. Then the #1 lift had a short in a safety switch and all the skiers had to be taken off by using the pony motor. As this was happening, we had a major accident on the #2 chair. One of the SMI guns got hooked by a chair, went around the top bull wheel, and derailed the cable. The only thing that saved the whole lift from coming down was the cable getting up on top of the chair track. Thankfully no one was injured.

December 25:
Merry Christmas. Clear and cold – good skiing – #2 top a bit thin but should have #2 bottoms, #1 and Beginners' Area open.

January 1:
Dennis broke the 2100 bulldozer – a key piece of equipment – again. This is the third time for him at a cost to HV of over $3,000 – he is not to drive any more. (Author's Note: Dennis eventually left HV and went to medical school. He is currently my family doctor. He continues to be active in National Ski Patrol but wisely leaves mountain maintenance to the maintenance crew.) Had right man on recovery pump all night, but did not get it fixed. Doug to Pennsylvania to pick up axle. Will not make snow until Sunday night. #2 in very bad shape. George came and gave us a list of 15 items that are wrong. Called Larry and he promised that he would be here on Monday and fix lift for sure this week.

January 2:
Still could not groom area because the 2100 and Sprite are both down. Skiing poor to fair to good.

January 5:
Excellent skiing – made snow first time in a week – we had largest crowd in history for non-Holiday week day.

January 8:
Excellent day. Members seem happy. Started making snow for #1 - made snow until 12:00; opened at 1:00 PM. And nothing broke!!!!!!!!!!!!!!

Once our first season was underway, ski operations may have caused behind the scenes stress, but our members seemed very pleased with their new ski club. On weekends and holidays, the Members' Lounge was always full of relaxed skiers. In accordance with Jack's vision, this section of the upper level of the lodge was reserved for members only. The area there was furnished with comfortable leather couches and chairs, and lovely Danish furniture.

Members loved their special perk. The Members' Lounge was always busy, at breakfast time, for coffee breaks and, best of all, for the ever-popular wine and cheese parties held at the end of the ski day. Unbeknownst to our happy members, the furniture company that sold us the lounge furniture kept hounding Hidden Valley to pay for the furniture we had purchased back in November. Unfortunately, we had not yet made enough profit to complete our end of the sales agreement.

One bright spring Sunday afternoon, a large Hertz rental truck pulled up to the lodge. Three men jumped out. They quickly went to the lounge and began to move the furniture down the stairs, out the front door and into the truck. The "movers" were polite. They repeatedly said, "Excuse me," as they asked the people to vacate their seats.

Relaxed occupants were appalled by the request, no matter how well couched. Since the movers were generally big burly guys, however, few members had the courage to protest. Meanwhile, we smiled our best PR smiles and tried to keep the members placated. One doubts whether anyone believed our hastily conceived explanation that newer, even nicer furniture would be delivered in a few days.

Once the Members' Lounge was emptied, one piece of furniture remained. This was a small three-shelf teak cabinet. When the other furniture was ordered, Jack had spotted that cabinet and paid for it with his personal American Express card. It was the only piece for which we had actually paid. The rest of the pieces were now in a Hertz rental truck on their way back to a Danish furniture store in Wayne.

Rather than leave a reminder of our newest calamity and accentuate the negative atmosphere of an all-but-empty Members Lounge, that evening the cabinet was quietly moved down to Jack's office, ever after to be used for storing papers, journals and used coffee cups. At least the clutter of Jack's wide ranging interests could then be kept to a minimum.

Jack's office was originally pretty Spartan, but soon it filled with odds and ends donated by the investors. Among the eclectic collection of donations were two legal office chairs, black with gold gilt trim and "Princeton University" outlined in bold lettering on their backs, a leather couch from the Kurlander home and several paintings and photos. The décor was definitely "early poverty". Who had time to worry about that?

Jack & mountain dog Chipper take a swim at Crystal Springs Quarry

Chipper takes mid day snooze at office in Hidden Valley..

Jack's office was always a popular stopping spot for friends to pop in to chat or socialize while they put on their ski boots. His office also was also the place where department heads came to discuss operational problems. High priority guests took advantage of the ready accessibility of the office and usually headed there to discuss everything from the weather and ski conditions to the latest problem with our government. Charlie Gibson from Good Morning America was a frequent visitor, hopping over from New York in a large limo from the GMA studio.

Jack's most frequent visitor, however, and his most loyal stress-reducer, was our dog, Chipper. Chipper quickly became the "Otto" of Hidden Valley. When he was not making the rounds and charming visitors, Chipper could be counted on to stop by daily for a little snooze on the leather couch.

Even with the calming presence of Chipper and the daily comradeship of his many friends who stopped by the office to chat, Jack soon bowed to the inevitable. The first season's cash flow at Hidden Valley was a disaster. Accounts payable rose and revenues fell throughout February and March. Hints of spring turned skiers' thoughts to golf, tennis and fishing.

Shortly after Hidden Valley ended its initial season in late March of 1976, Jack called an emergency meeting of the Hidden Valley Board of Directors to discuss the situation. As part of their membership agreement, each investor who joined the organization was automatically eligible to be a member of the Board of Directors and was given a seat on the Hidden Valley Board. In addition to being a stockholder hoping for a return on his investment, each received lifetime skiing privileges for himself and his family. An added incentive to invest was the promise of a building lot on the mountain, which would be made available once the access road was complete and subdivision approvals obtained. So, naturally, the Board members were as concerned as we about Hidden Valley's future.

Most of the investors were there in the lodge when Jack arrived to open the meeting. With his usual sense of humor and air of optimism, he started off with the following words:

"Gentlemen, thank you for attending today. I have some good news and some bad news. First, the good news. In our large walk-in freezers are a number of beautiful, frozen, fully-cooked 29-pound, choice prime rib roasts which each of you will take home today. These are being given to all of you to show our gratitude for your supports this past year."

The news was received with enthusiasm. Everyone was standing, smiling, cheering and clapping. Jack continued:

"Now the bad news. The reason you are each receiving these beautiful, frozen, fully cooked, 29-pound, choice Prime Rib Roasts is that the Sussex Rural Power & Light Company is coming tomorrow to shut off the electricity at Hidden Valley."

Mouths gaped open followed by utter silence. Hidden Valley was broke. The Board voted for economy. Staff was cut to a bare minimum. With the exception of a few outside maintenance employees and key office people, everyone worked without pay. The Board, however, also agreed to finish the tennis courts and pool so efforts could be redoubled to sell summer memberships.

Shortly after the infamous emergency Board meeting, August Arace, a frequent skier at Hidden Valley, approached Jack and indicated that he would like to join the investor team. Once they agreed that August (Augie) would make a commitment to invest in the ski area, Jack and Augie decided to meet for lunch at a small restaurant in East Orange to finalize details.

The day of their meeting was a hectic one for Jack. That morning, the bookkeeper met with Jack and reported that funds were desperately needed to pay some important bills – mainly for the gas company, the Sussex Rural Electric Company and silly little things like that. Jack drove to East Orange in our 1963 lime green Fiat. It badly needed a new muffler. He seemed to attract used vehicles with muffler problems. The car banged and back fired on the hour-long trip to the meeting. He arrived in "high stress mode."

The two men ordered their food and began to discuss Augie's investment. Jack was enjoying his favorite French onion soup. Suddenly he passed out and did a Goldie Hawn nose dive into the soup. Augie shouted for someone to call the rescue squad. I am not sure back then if 911 was in effect. I do know the ambulance arrived promptly and the rescue squad rushed Jack to East Orange General Hospital.

Augie called with the bad news. I immediately drove to the hospital where I was pleased to see Augie and Jack's dear friend, John Cassidy. John and Judy, the two of our children then in New Jersey, hurried to join me at the hospital. Jack was being kept stable by assorted tubes and lots of breathing apparatus and IV's. I went to his bedside, held his hand and said: "I'm here honey. Don't worry! You are going to be fine".

Jack opened his eyes and said, "I have never cheated on you and am so happy to have you as my life partner." He then breathed heavily and uttered in a very soft voice, "Get the check . . . to the bank." In my most reassuring voice, I tried to restore calm. I kept repeating, "Don't worry. I'll go there now. It will be deposited today." He breathed a sigh of relief, closed his eyes and prepared for what was to be a very long recovery. I ran to the bank and deposited the check.

Jack's primary care doctor and long standing friend, Dr. Lucian Fletcher, took over control via direct contact with the nurse's station at the hospital. Soon afterward Lucian called to alert me to the fact that Jack was being rushed to the highly regarded Heart and Trauma Center at Newark's Beth Israel Hospital.

Jack was moved into the Beth Israel operating room at midnight. We spent the next ten hours waiting and receiving regular reports on the progress. It was the longest day of my life. Miraculously, he slowly began to improve. As we had learned the hard way, minimizing stress when your business is running an under-funded new ski area in northwest New Jersey is difficult to impossible.

Peg Takes Over

Two months later, Jack was transferred to Newton Hospital to be closer to home. After three more months of rehab, he returned home for further rest and modest exercise. During that period, he decided that he would not return to running a ski area in New Jersey or anywhere else. He just could not imagine going back to the daily stress the job placed on him.

To solve the current leadership crisis, the Board met and asked if I would take over Jack's position. The challenge of running the company would be an unusual one for a forty-year-old woman at work in an industry run almost exclusively by men. Reluctantly, I agreed to take over the reins. Despite my doubts, this turned out to be one of the most rewarding experiences of my life. Changing the structure of the Board was one of my first problems to solve.

Our existing Hidden Valley Board of Directors was bigger than the one at General Motors. I decided we needed to form an Executive Committee to make the decisions that the more cumbersome Board of Directors was too large to handle efficiently. We restructured our charter and formed the more workable Executive Committee. This unique and wonderful group of men each brought his perspectives and talents to the table. They deserve much credit for guiding me through the tough times that lay ahead. The original eight-man committee also deserves credit for Hidden Valley's turnaround and its ultimate survival.

One of the first investors selected was Augie Arace, who, having been a stockbroker for many years, brought us his strong background in finance. Larry Marchiony's contribution came primarily from his experience in the advertising/public relations field. A man of many talents, Larry also did the oil painting of the trail map which still hangs in the lodge to this day. Don Decker brought us his business acumen and experience in the computer industry. Jim Kittel continued to oversee the accounting department. Joe Riggs helped bring quality programs and fun skiing to Hidden Valley. Joerg Speck took over the Mountain Manager position while, at the same time, supervising the food and beverage departments. Bill Evans continued to serve as the company attorney. Finally, Jack Murphy contributed his architectural skills wherever needed.

The Executive Committee met once a month to revise budgets and become knowledgeable about all aspects of the operations. What an incredible experience for me to be working with this talented group. They taught me so much about finance and a host of other things. Some of the members of the committee have told me that these were the best years of their lives. Everyone, including me, felt we were living a dream.

At that time, my management skills were pretty limited so I decided on a simple strategy. When preparing spread sheets estimating profit and loss, I always estimated very low income and overestimated outgo. Every month, the board thought I was a genius for running a very tight ship. It was tight all right, but they always seemed happy to hear that income had exceeded the budgeted numbers and that expenses were lower than projected. That worked for about our first six months. The formula I had created seemed to keep everyone less stressed about our future.

One of our early meetings that I recall with a bit of humor was anything but stress free. One evening, the Executive Committee met in the New Jersey Bank building on Route 80 near the Paterson exit. The meeting took place in the conference room of the 12th floor where our attorneys had their offices. The meeting had just begun when the power went off throughout the building. None of us was familiar with the layout of the offices. We needed some light. We groped our way around until someone found some matches and an inter-office building phone. Someone called the security number and explained who we were and how we had come to be locked in the bank. We all had to give our names and Social Security numbers before a guard would come up to guide us down the twelve flights and out of the bank. The building had kicked into automatic lock-down. What an unforgettable experience. I am not sure that any important decisions were made that night. I do know we never again met at the New Jersey Bank building.

From the first, the new Executive Committee agreed with me that we must continue to keep staff at a bare minimum, but still complete work on the upper valley so as to attract summer revenue. Somehow or other, I managed to get through the summer and into the second season at Hidden Valley, 1976-1977, with the capable help of my small but willing staff.

Helen took care of administrative duties. In addition to supervising the kitchen, Joerg agreed to continue to oversee work on the mountain. A small group of mechanics and equipment operators agreed to stay on and help him. Jim continued with money matters.

Most of us worked pro bono in hopes of holding things together until revenues picked up. Money was simply not available.

From the day I took over, our needs were pretty obvious. To continue to operate, we needed to borrow money somewhere. The Executive Committee met and called the entire Board for another special meeting. I announced that we needed more money to keep things going and that I needed a capital infusion ASAP. The following week, the Board met again. This time I announced that it was not a matter of would they lend the money, but rather that they MUST. Most of the investors quickly put in the funds we needed to stay afloat. A few investors, however, indicated they were not able or willing and favored folding Hidden Valley.

Jim and Jorge took large cuts in pay and worked for very limited salaries. We assured them that the shortfall would be paid to them when things improved. Cutting salaries seemed to be the only way that the company could limp along and reopen for the second season. Most everyone was in agreement on this, although a few investors still objected to our efforts to keep going.

My struggle to keep my own household going also required sacrifices. Soon, I had to take money from our emergency savings. One day, a car pulled up to my home. A man knocked on the door and without any comment, handed me a check. This procedure continued for many months. A check was hand-delivered every Friday.

We never discussed who was writing the check, what the obligations were or how we were to repay this money. This was truly an anonymous transaction. I was able to pay the household bills and help the patient through the ordeal. I have an inkling of who our benefactor was, but revealing the name would be a breach of that person's privacy.

Later that first summer, the tennis courts and the pool were finished and sales efforts to attract more members began to pay off. Operations went smoothly. Equipment was not breaking down as it had the first year. Equally important, this marked the start of some very good snow years. With members of the Executive Committee serving as my mentors and sounding boards, the bottom line improved. Augie often mentioned that they attended the committee meetings each month so that they could "vote to do what Peggy says to do". One of the ski trails at Hidden Valley was later named Pegasus (Peg-as-us or

Peggy Says), probably a subtle play on words for which no one yet takes credit. Of course, things were not always rosy, but we managed to stumble through. Security at night was important. We found we needed to hire a night watchman. Our search for a man to be on the site daily ended with the hiring of a man named Joe and his large German shepherd, aptly named Wolf. We often wondered about our watchman's "trained dog". Was he a trained watchdog, a trained attack dog or just a plain old wolf? Regardless, I made sure to leave the lodge as soon as they arrived. I do not know if the dog was ever turned loose at Hidden Valley. I really do not want to know.

One night, I had a funny feeling about the lodge security. I asked Jack to drive me back to the lodge so I could personally check on things. When we arrived, we unlocked the door and went in. Joe was not there! We looked everywhere for the dog and his trainer without success. I called the security guard at his home and he answered the phone. I blew my stack. He rushed over to the lodge. In typical Donald Trump style, I shouted, "You're fired." We escorted the guard to the door, took his keys and booted him out the door.

A few minutes later he was back, knocking on the door and signaling to me. I went over to hear what he was attempting to say. "Could you punch me out on my time card?" Guess he rather naively wanted to make sure he was going to be paid for the evening!

At the start of the second season, I sought a lodge manager who could take over staff supervision, lodge mechanicals and any other problems arising at the clubhouse. We approached Gary Kitchell, a young tennis pro friend, who readily accepted the position. From his first day on the job, Gary made Hidden Valley a fun place to work. As an added bonus, his wife Marie Elena ran the ticket desk on the nights that Gary was on duty. This family affair worked well for all of us.

A subtle behind-the-scenes decision, when running a large public area such as the lodge, is what kind of music, if any, should play in the background. My idea was always to have soothing classical music piped throughout the lodge, thereby fostering a peaceful attitude for our skiers. The classics were the standard music played daily throughout the lodge. Every night, of course, after we had left for home, the sound system was pumped up. This was done with Gary's approval to please the teen-age and young adult skiers and spectators. We pretended we did not know of the change in the atmosphere at Hidden Valley after we had left. Even though the noise level accelerated nightly, our night managers kept things under control. Gary and Maria Elena, being much younger than myself and Jack, were willing to compromise in order to keep the customers happy.

Like Jack, Gary was a type-A personality who, in a burst of enthusiasm, often rushed about, accidentally banging into doors and overhead beams. Gary was a great story teller and loved an audience. His stories were legendary. One was especially dramatic. One time, when driving to work from his home in Sparta, he was delayed by an injured deer blocking the road. Hidden Valley depended on his being on the job. He had no other choice but to dash from his car, pocket knife in hand, and begin immediately to euthanize the doomed animal.

After a year on the job at Hidden Valley, Gary went back to school to study physical therapy. He soon became one of the finest physical therapists in Sussex County. Today, he is better known as a trainer, working with famous tennis pros including Ivan Lendl and John McEnroe.

In the years he worked for me at Hidden Valley, Gary was a very comforting, protective force. One night, Gary stopped by the lodge to check on a few things. As he unlocked the door and walked into the office, he noticed that the door to the money room was standing ajar. Two teen-age boys were busily trying to break into the very large safe which was secured to the floor of the room.

The boys dashed out of the lodge with Gary in hot pursuit. He found the thieves hiding behind the maintenance building, dragged them back into the lodge and called the police. The thieves turned out to be a group of teenagers who were stealing keys, breaking into lockers and making off with whatever they could find. The boys were sent on to juvenile court. To the best of my knowledge, they never again caused trouble at our area.

On another very busy evening, two customers came to the front desk to report that their skis had just been stolen from the racks in front of the lodge. Some of the stolen skis were from our rental shop. Gary hurried out to the parking lot in time to see a car full of teenagers hurrying in suspicious haste out onto to the road. He chased them as far as he could without success and then reported the theft to the Vernon Police.

Several weeks later I received a call from a man who owned an ice cream parlor in Warwick, New York. He told me about four teenagers who frequently came into his shop. The boys had confessed their guilt to this trusted confidant. They regretted what they had done and wanted to return the skis. He asked me that if the skis were returned, would we be willing to forego pressing charges. I called our attorney, Bill Evans. Bill's advice was "Get the skis. If you don't, they will end up at the bottom of some river or lake."

We set a date for the manager/friend to accompany the boys when they came to Hidden Valley to return the skis. The guilty boys appeared to be roughly 16-19 years of age. I began by reading them my little lecture about integrity and honesty.

Meantime, two of my burliest and fiercest looking mechanics, Hap and Freddy, were waiting outside the door to my office. I guess they were concerned about my safety. How reassuring for me to have them there awaiting a call to come meet the culprits. I invited my two protectors to come inside and introduced the boys to Hap and Freddy. Then I asked the men to stand in front of the boys and get a good look at their faces.

Hap and Freddy stood there in their finest grease-monkey coveralls, holding in their hands the large wrenches they routinely used to open and shut pipes on the mountain. I instructed my escorts, "If you ever see them on the premises at Hidden Valley in the future, you have my permission to take them behind the pump house and beat the * * * * out of them." After the skis were secured, I sighed with relief. I am confident that these boys never pulled a stunt like that again. I wish them the best of luck in life and trust facing up to a guilty act was a valuable lesson.

Even with Gary around to lighten the load, my job was full of challenging tests. The worst of the catastrophes I lived through at Hidden Valley, or at least of the ones which the Mountain Men told me about, was when an operating snow gun disconnected and jammed a chair on the chairlift, causing a derailment. This triggered a shut-down alert, which automatically stopped the lift. The night of the derailment, the lift was fully loaded with skiers. One by one, the ski patrollers hitched safety straps around their waists and climbed the lift towers. Once on top of the towers, they helped the skiers put on safety jackets and assisted in their descent. To anxious cheers on my part, they managed to get everyone down safely.

Thankfully, our patrol was well prepared to handle this emergency. The ski patrollers were quite pleased to have the opportunity to use their practiced skills. Our Mountain Manager and I were not so pleased with the snowmaking crew that night. Most likely they were not performing their jobs correctly. Snowmakers work on the mountain mostly at night through tough conditions including wind, snow or freezing rain. Their pay is not much, considering the difficulty of the job. The factors leading to the derailment, however, were not acceptable.

A year or so later, a cable on the Chicken Delight beginner area derailed, causing skiers some terrifying minutes. Some kids had been bouncing up and down on the chair, causing skis and an empty chair to land hard on the snow below. This also set up a jam on the lift and necessitated evacuating that lift. Score two for the patrol, who again got everyone down safely. I think they really began to enjoy their jobs as rescue heroes.

Let me add a few words here about safety at ski areas. Although a few accidents have happened at ski areas across the county, most of the time these accidents are caused by high winds. To be on the cautious side, I, for one, do not recommend taking high and long lift rides on those days. Ski areas routinely post instructions as to what to do if evacuating from a lift is necessary. Hopefully, this never happens on your watch.

Throughout my days managing Hidden Valley, looking for ways to operate more economically was always important. This meant considering every idea, no matter how improbable. My experiment in animal husbandry and agronomy was one of my more extreme measures. When I took over, I noted that a lot of time and money was spent mowing the grass and underbrush in the base area near the triple chairlift.

My solution was to ask Horace Theobold, a local farmer, if he would let Hidden Valley borrow two of his goats to see if they could keep these areas "grazed" and groomed. We attached the goats to cinder blocks and moved the blocks from time to time to even out the grazing taking place around the base area.

Three days after the experiment was started, some of the men told me that the two goats had fallen into a hole under the counter weight below the lift. Both animals had strangled. I felt terrible about this unforeseen calamity. How, I pondered, was I to confess this major miscalculation to Horace?

That day, I ordered two new goats and had them delivered to Horace's farm. I promised the Mountain Men that I would never try that stupid trick again. Apparently, a cost-cutting program of designated grazing was not one of my better efforts.

On the other hand, I cherish a few unexpected successes. Hidden Valley was always looking for billboard space to promote our area. One good location we knew of could be seen on Route 517. It had been previously leased by Vernon Valley. Evidently, someone forgot to renew the lease. The owners of the billboard were approached and we signed a two year lease. After the Hidden Valley sign was installed, a call was made to Gene Mulvihill and I asked if he had any other signs he was not planning to renew.

Of course, Gene had delegated those marketing and advertising tasks to some of his employees. He did not know a thing about the sign situation. My call was made in the true spirit of gamesmanship. Score one for the little guy! Needless to say, thereafter, the Vernon Valley marketing department double checked the status of all their billboard locations.

Ski Conditions and Ski Writers

One of my jobs at both Great Gorge and Hidden Valley involved passing on the daily ski conditions to radio and newspaper personnel, who counted on these reports as part of their job. A ski conditions report was always a lesson

Peg gives official morning report at Hidden Valley

"Peg, will you answer the phone and give the ski report!"

in creativity and it always depended upon the weather. After a four-foot snow storm, the report was easy. Just take a ruler and stick it in a set place near the lodge, check with the local weather station to confirm how much snow had fallen overnight and what the temperature was in the morning.

A rainfall, followed by a quick freeze, presented its own challenge. Each morning, the Mountain Manager and groomers reported to me the conditions on the mountain and what had been "groomed," meaning chopped up and dragged around by a long chain. Today's expensive and high-tech grooming machines do a fabulous job. They are a welcome relief when compared to the machinery we had in the 1960's and 1970's. Back then, grooming status reports were very tricky to handle. Rainfall predicted for the afternoon was also a challenge.

My responsibility was to answer my home phone when ski reporters called to get information for their morning radio shows. Often Jack and I were both sound asleep when a call came in. Jack usually nudged me to remind me that I had to give the morning ski report. I became very proficient at glancing out

"And now for the forecast for the next week at Hidden Valley"

the window to see if it was clear, raining or snowing and, at the same time, checking the indoor/outdoor thermometer, all while remembering the weather report from the night before. These calculations were usually done between 4:00 and 5:00am, and I was almost always ready by the time I answered the phone.

Most of the time, my make-shift methods were pretty accurate – all this being before the up-to-the-minute weather reports on The Weather Channel that we now take for granted. Having today's laptop computer beside my bed would have been very helpful.

One of my favorite ski reporters was Stan Bernard, who covered most of the areas in the northeast by making phone calls in the wee hours of the morning. Stan and I would begin with a short chat about the kids and assorted family news and then move on to the reporting. Another favorite was Roxie Rothefeld, who called only on Thursday and Friday mornings. Roxie became such a regular caller that we often kiddingly talked about making a date to ski some place in Vermont or to test out some of the "big mountains" far removed from our humbler New Jersey slopes.

Other ski writers covered more than weather conditions. They often sought me out for feature news stories about what was going on at the area. They sometimes traded a day of skiing for a positive write up, and most stayed on to become first-name friends. These business-related friendships lasted over many years. Alas, most of my favorite ski reporters are now off skiing in some snowy cloud in the sky. I remember, fondly, Alan Macaulay of the Bergen Record, Red Hoffman from the Newark News, Jerry Kinney of the New York Daily News and Bill Katterman of the Star Ledger. These columnists did so much to popularize skiing. Unfortunately, most of the ski writers of today are the victims of recessionary cutbacks and the declining circulation of newspapers in the United States. Most skiers now get their data from their iPhones and Droids. These sources may be very efficient. They fail, however, to lure us with the charm and aura of commentary that those early ski reporters never failed to impart.

The Battle of the Sexes

Hidden Valley Swim and Tennis Club needed more members to help defray the costs of running the tennis courts and maintaining the grounds. The staff thought up some incentives to encourage new membership. I came up with a unique promotion – The Battle of the Sexes. Many readers will remember the famous tennis duel between Billie Jean King and Bobby Riggs. In 1973, Billie Jean had won six Wimbledon singles championships, four US Open titles, and was ranked #1 in the world. Riggs, a 1939 Wimbledon champion turned hustler, had already massacred Margaret Court earlier that year in Houston on Mother's Day. King was motivated to get revenge for women and agreed to accept Riggs' challenge.

The 1973 Battle of the Sexes captured the imagination of the country, not just tennis enthusiasts. Billy Jean entered the Texas Astrodome Court like Cleopatra, in a gold litter held aloft by four muscular men dressed as ancient slaves. Riggs was wheeled in on a rickshaw pulled by sexy models in tight outfits with shirts monogrammed with "Bobby's Bosom Buddies". The extravaganza ended with Billie Jean winning 6-4, 6-3 and 6-3.

Our Hidden Valley Battle of the Sexes, that took place a few years later, was a little different. During a lively evening at the George Inn, a group of us sat at tables next to a group of Playboy time-share salesmen who were partying, singing and enjoying lots of beer. Pretty soon, our small group joined the singing and hoisted our own mugs filled with Guinness. One thing led to another. Small talk ensued about what people did for a living. I, of course, told them about Hidden Valley and the new Swim and Tennis Club. We were looking for new members.

One of the salesmen said that he loved to play tennis. I encouraged him to take a $500 membership for the summer months. He replied by suggesting that we play a tennis match. If he lost, the Hidden Valley Club would receive a check covering the $500. We then agreed that if he won, I would pay with a $500 check payable to my favorite charity.

The next morning, I called a few friends to find out if this guy was hot air or was a good player. One friend said, "I don't know anything about his tennis ability, Peg. I do know that a time-share salesman never makes a bet that he thinks he is going to lose." My hopes dwindled rapidly.

The match was scheduled for 10:00am. I arrived half an hour early and noticed a lot of chairs set up in the indoor tennis courts at Playboy. News had travelled fast. A large number of people had heard about the challenge. The chairs were quickly filling up with spectators anxious to see Hidden Valley's Battle of the Sexes.

The salesman, Jim, arrived wearing some very scuffed and dirty tennis shoes and a very tired warm-up suit. He carried a very old Wilson wood tennis racket. I had dressed in my cutest tennis dress, hoping that would be a diversion. Warm up time came. I fed him some balls, which were hit back so hard I could feel them zooming past my side. I was worried.

The traditional coin toss took place. He elected to receive, and I felt a glimmer of hope. Maybe he did not have confidence in his serve. My first serve was returned to me so fast that I never saw the ball. This was repeated for the rest of that first game. We then changed sides. His serves were such that I could not get near them to return. Now I was in big trouble.

At this point, I noted that he was perspiring profusely and his face was very red. I realized that all I had to do was to keep the ball in play and not worry about how hard he might hit the ball. Despite the early bravado, he began to gasp and limp around. Amid much cheering and excitement, the match ended in my favor. I won easily by the score of 6-2, 6-0.

We headed back to the George Inn to finish up the $500 bet arrangement. I happily recovered my check, payable to my charity, and his check, made out to Hidden Valley. The next day, he called and asked that I hold the check for two days to be sure it would clear. The bad news was that his checking account had been closed. The good news was that he left town, never to be seen again. In spite of not receiving the money, I still enjoy telling the story about the Hidden Valley Battle of the Sexes. I also learned not to take the word of a Playboy salesman!!!!!

One of my saddest days at Hidden Valley occurred the following winter, on Christmas morning in 1978. That day still lingers in my mind. Nancy, the daughter of my secretary, Helen, worked on weekends at the front desk. She was a very capable young lady and came to work early that morning to help me get things going for the day. The phone rang at the front desk and Nancy answered. She was shocked to hear a Vernon Police officer advise that her mother had an asthma attack and was being rushed to one of the local hospitals. A half hour later another policeman called to inform us that Helen did not respond to resuscitation and had passed away. Everyone was completely devastated by the loss of this very admired and capable woman.

A week or two later, I had run an ad for an executive secretary to help me run the business. One of the applicants was Linda Kroeger, who called and received an interview. I liked everything about her – an easy laugh, intelligence and excellent skills. The next morning when I arrived at my office, I found a letter on my desk from Linda. She won me over when she added in her closing note, "I enjoyed meeting you yesterday and want to tell you I would be thrilled and pleased to take the position. As a matter of fact, I want the job so badly I can taste it." She started work the following week and continued to work at Hidden Valley for a number of years, even for several years after I retired. In addition to being a fine administrator, she also has become one of my dearest friends.

New Buyer for Hidden Valley

I continued to manage Hidden Valley for a total of nine years. Even after Jack was fully recovered from his heart attack, he was content to have me remain as manager. Jack decided to accept Gene Mulvihill's offer to work on such special projects as the Stonehill development next to The Spa and to explore other projects that might be done on his own.

An exit strategy was needed. Selling my part of the business meant exiting from both management and/or stockholder ownership. Frequent meetings with Bill Evans were held, with the emphasis on planning how to sell the area. Discussions ranged from where the company could expect to expand in the future to how to run the company more efficiently.

We both wanted to sell our interest in Hidden Valley, but wanted to be sure that all the stockholders would have a choice of whether to stay on or to sell their interest. Bill tried to draw a profile of who might want to own a ski area. He envisioned a country gentleman, dressed in tweed coat with a natty look. He would have to love skiing, business, outdoor activities and perhaps have an interest in ski racing for his children. Of course, most important was that this hypothetical person be financially able to make the purchase.

Two brothers were current investors. They had also been investors in Great American Recreation, which operated the Vernon Valley Ski Area. They skied, had successful business interests, had kids and had built ski houses on the mountain. After a number of meetings, however, it became apparent that they were not interested.

Several months later, one of the current Hidden Valley investors indicated he wanted to purchase the entire property including the real estate, the summer club and the ski area with all its assets. He offered to buy out all the stockholders. This would not be a condition of the purchase. If current stockholders decided to remain as investors, they were free to do so. They could also keep the perks that went along with membership, including free lifetime skiing for the investor and his family.

The prospective buyer was Donald Begraft, the man who had built the condominiums at Hidden Valley. Now, Begraft hoped to expand in two areas. He wanted to upgrade the summer facilities, including the pool, the picnic areas and tennis courts. He also planned to improve the food service areas. Everyone was happy with the transaction. I was comfortable and agreed to stay on until a new General Manager was found. The transition went smoothly.

At this period in 1982, the Canadian company, Intrawest, had just purchased the Vernon Valley/Great Gorge properties. They brought in a massive infusion of funds to expand ski lifts and trails, and build a hotel. They also began to develop that area's residential real estate. Real estate prices in those years were rising at an astonishing rate. The boom times were here. This was a good time for me to retire, and to spend more time with family and enjoy a more leisurely life style. (And this time around, selling our interests in a ski area generated some profit.)

The Ultimate Compliment

On my last day as General Manager, I was clearing out my desk. A knock came at the door and I was surprised to see Freddie Ohmen. We chatted for a few minutes. Freddie came over to my desk and gave me a big hug.

Freddie, with very fine theatrical farewell, said, "Peg, I never thought I would be able to work for a woman, but I must say, you did a hell of a job!"

AMEN

Evening beauty of the Lodge at Hidden Valley

The boss gets full Patrol service after a wrong turn at Great Gorge

Jamie & Judy on mats in the summertime

– CHAPTER 16 –

THE VERNON VALLEY/ GREAT GORGE YEARS

The following passages consist of information solicited from various sources in the Great Gorge/Vernon Valley administrative offices and from background information belonging to the author. The chapter is included here because it flushes out our story and hopefully will be of interest to the reader. Please note that some parts of the Vernon Valley story are incomplete because once the Kurlanders were bought out of Great Gorge they were no longer involved with the ski operations or the merger with Great American Recreation that followed shortly afterwards. Much of the information about Vernon Valley, and ultimately the Vernon Valley/Great Gorge ski area from this point onward, the author obtained by talking with friends and employees who did work there. Other information was obtained from press clippings and matters of public record. Also, be aware that Vernon was still a small town in the 1970's. Back then, when so many residents were on a first-name basis, everyone seemed to know everything about everyone.

In an earlier chapter, I described how Jack Kurlander found property at Hamburg Mountain suitable for building a major ski resort area in Vernon, New Jersey. His dreams became reality when he opened the Great Gorge Ski Area in 1965. The lower part of Hamburg Mountain had been owned privately. The top of the mountain was owned by the State of New Jersey. Jack realized that the top of the mountain would also be needed to achieve his plan to develop major mountain status. The top of the mountain became a key factor for Great Gorge and for the future of skiing in Sussex County.

When the Great Gorge Ski Area opened for skiing in 1965, its success was immediate. Skiers from New York, New Jersey and Pennsylvania were anxious to test their skills at the new ski area. During the next few years, new lifts, trails, improved snowmaking and trail grooming were added. Lift ticket revenue increased rapidly. By December of 1972, Great Gorge had expanded and opened a new section of the mountain known as Great Gorge North. North had its own lifts and trails and was linked to the South area by a separate lift and trail at the top of the mountain complex. Across the valley, the Playboy Club opened a new hotel in February of 1972 and it was expected that it would bring even more skiers.

When Great Gorge first went into operation, the area was open seven days and three nights a week and closed between the day and evening ski sessions to groom the slopes for the night skiers. Continued growth of Great Gorge soon dictated that the ski area would open at 9:00am and operate until 10:00pm.

The importance of obtaining a lease to use the upper property at Great Gorge came into play in the future development of Great Gorge and the history of the area. The State of New Jersey, through their Department of Fish and Game, mandated that anyone who wished to have use of the top of the mountain would be required to have an approved lease.

After Jack finished his plans, showing how the mountain would be developed, he made an appointment to meet with Robert Roe, Commissioner of the New Jersey Conservation and Economic Development. Part of Bob's job as Commissioner was to oversee the activities of the State Division of Fish and Game and covered wildlife control and land usage. Jack knew that this upper property was needed. He knew that approvals from all departments were necessary. In 1964, Jack again met with Commissioner Roe who agreed with Jack that a major ski area in McAfee would be beneficial for the State financially, and environmentally and would be compatible within the guidelines set by the Division of Fish and Game. A lease was signed with the State and further planning for the mountain top became a high priority.

The first phase of development at Great Gorge included all the lower mountain lifts and trails. Two years later, a chairlift from Base Area to the Summit was installed. Other lifts and trails, including the Racing Trail, were added later.

In 1967, while skiing at Great Gorge, a group of men from Staten Island were impressed by the success of Great Gorge. They decided that building another ski area on Hamburg Mountain would also be a smart investment for them. They learned that they also needed to obtain top of the mountain permits. They went to Trenton to see if they could also get a lease for the top of Hamburg Mountain. Sometime that year, this group, now called Vernon Valley, was also granted a lease. We can find no record of any economic, environmental or other feasibility studies performed to see if this was an appropriate action. No hearings are on record to show whether or not that, in approving this second ski area, the State was creating unfair competition for the relatively new Great Gorge. Nor, as far as we know, were studies ever made to see if the proposed usage of the Vernon Valley property was compatible with the State's mission to protect its existing wildlife. Additionally, studies were never done to show the availability of water, the impact on sewerage systems and treatment plants, or the impact that increased traffic to the area would have on existing state and county roads.

As a side note of interest, here is the way times have changed since the 1960's. If a group wanted to build another ski area in Vernon today, it would take approvals from the town, county and State. It is estimated that this process would take five years. Regardless, the State of New Jersey issued a lease to the newly proposed Vernon Valley Ski Area, which was constructed and opened in 1968.

The consequences were almost immediate. In a very short period of time, the competition between the two ski areas affected both. As part of its original lease agreement, Great Gorge paid the State of New Jersey a fee based on the number of lift tickets sold each month. The State and the ski area were, in essence, partners. Once a competing ski area opened next door, however, this partnership agreement began to create great difficulties for Great Gorge. It affected the ability to pay the lease fees and cover its other financial obligations. As the old saying goes, "With friends like this, who needs enemies?"

The story for Vernon Valley was fraught with danger. Soon after construction started, the three original Vernon investors ran out of money and two more investors, who had control over a small publicly traded company, were brought in. This expanded group fared no better and had to borrow more money again. This time, they borrowed money from a group of Wall Street investors which included Henry Neuworth and Gene Mulvihill. Gene was the one in the group who knew how to ski and he was designated to check things out. He checked with Jack and discussed a plan for putting together the two ski areas. Gene suggested that he would raise money from Wall Street and they would merge. Jack took the idea back to his partners who were not at all interested in accepting this plan. Out of funds, the partners were out the door. Even before the official merger took place, a key job change colored everything that followed. Charlie O'Brien, the Mountain Manager from Great Gorge and its most valued employee, was named CEO of the new entity. Noted in some of the amusing stories in our earlier chapter on Great Gorge's Mountain Men, Charlie was a hard-drinking ex-Marine gunnery sergeant who ably ran our snow-making operations. This is the same fun-loving Charlie O'Brien who appears in the "Otto Mountain Dog" story, capturing my white cat every year on St. Patrick's Day and coloring it Irish green.

Charlie commanded intense loyalty from all the men who worked for him at Great Gorge. Gene Mulvihill was a former captain in the Marines and, once introduced to the head snowmaker at Great Gorge, immediately hit it off with Charlie. So what happened? The two Marines joined together and all the men followed Charlie to Vernon Valley. This, it is alleged, is what finally forced the Kaufmans to make a deal to turn things over to Vernon Valley. What is known is, as soon as the newly merged Vernon Valley/Great Gorge was in control of the whole mountain. Mulvihill and O'Brien immediately cut new trails to connect the two mountains. Most people thought that Mulvihill was crazy, leaving a guy like Charlie O'Brien in charge of both ski areas. Charlie may not

Charlie O'Brien & aide test Curtiss Wright jet engine for snowmaking

have been the best Mountain Manager on the planet but he surely could make snow better than anyone. He was not an executive and had no executive experience. Nevertheless, he was named President of the Corporation and was put in charge of everything. The thing about Charlie was that everybody loved him. He had always inspired tremendous loyalty from his men, and the men who worked for him were wonderful workers. Great Gorge/Vernon Valley was closed for unknown reasons in 1996 and 1997 but was back up and running in 1998. (That information can probably be found on Google or other internet sources.) This time around, it was purchased by the Canadian Company known as Intrawest and the ski area was reopened under its current name of Mountain Creek.

Long before these events occurred, however, other equally influential events were taking place that reshaped the entire recreational direction of our quiet little valley. Faced with the challenge to maintain revenues, ski areas everywhere began to add summer recreation activities. The owners of Vernon Valley decided that the best solution was to add some sort of summer amusement park. There was one problem – the town had an ordinance against amusement rides and amusement rides in parks. At that time, the town was not exactly friendly to business I am told. Mulvihill made a clever decision. He decided that Vernon Valley would put in do-it-yourself attractions which were not really amusement rides but more like sporting attractions. The winter mountain was transformed into what was dubbed Action Park. The first of its wildly popular summer attractions was the Alpine Slide. The Alpine Slide was like a summer bobsled, a sled with wheels and runners that came down on concrete rather than a snowy trough. Next, the Great American group added Go-Karts, water slides and other do-it-yourself attractions such as wild river rides and nature pools cut right out of the side of the mountain with giant waterfalls--the likes of which no water park had ever seen. Tarzan swings dunked swingers into mountain ponds. Waterslides shot sliders through the air into mountain streams. The company also built a gigantic wave pool, a track for real Lola race cars and another waterway for racing speedboats. Next came bungee jumping and an air stream with a giant propeller that shot experienced flyers as high as 100 feet into the air. Action Park even had a marching band, fantastic shows including Broadway and Rock & Roll shows, and jousting competitions between individuals trying to knock one another off pedestals. From its earliest summer in 1978, Action Park was an instant success. Before long, Action Park was such a huge success that as many as 20,000 to 25,000 people were known to show up on some of its bigger days.

• •

After the ski areas merged and our direct involvement with the management of Vernon Valley and Great Gorge had ended, we faced the question of "now what"? Our family continued to live on the mountain at Great Gorge for a number of years. As we will see in the chapters that follow, Jack turned to starting another ski area nearby at Hidden Valley and from there to building summer activities at the new Crystal Springs Swim and Tennis Club.

We adjusted to our altered life style – still listening to skiers laughing and enjoying the outdoors as they skied by our chalet. Listening to snow guns at night was always a distraction from the peace and quiet one might expect living in our small mountain chalet.

In the summer, Vernon Valley/Great Gorge began to offer many activities and promotions. One of the big summer attractions was a huge Rock and Roll concert series to be held in the base area at the Gorge. On the day of the first scheduled concert, loudspeakers screamed all day and well into the night. The noise was overwhelming. Before the day of the first concert, we had talked to area management (that means Gene) about having the event closed by 10:00pm so that we and other mountain residents could get some sleep. When the night of the first concert arrived, we called the lodge several times to let them know the music was too loud and it was time for a curfew to be enforced. When that did not work, we called Gene at home shortly after 10:00pm. We let Gene know that we had had enough and even called the police to ask them to enforce the existing Vernon Township Noise Ordinance. Five minutes later, the music stopped, the P.A. system was turned off and attendees were quickly and quietly moved to the parking lots. I think Gene probably read the riot act to the employees who probably had never heard of a Noise Ordinance.

As time for the next concert neared, I approached Mulvihill and told him that we would take the issue of noise to the appropriate Township authorities and would cite the local noise ordinance laws which, in effect, prohibited excessive noise in the late evening hours. To our knowledge no one in Vernon Township had ever before challenged the legality or enforcement of this law. We told Gene that we had no other choice but to make the town aware of our opposition to the upcoming concert on the grounds of excessive noise. The residents wanted an early curfew at any concerts or events held at Great Gorge. Gene negotiated an acceptable solution to the problem.

Management offered to send the Kurlanders and the Fitzgeralds to Pennsylvania to a quiet resort hotel in the Poconos where we would have three days of an all-expense-paid vacation including food, beverage and golf. We had a great time in the Poconos that weekend knowing that Vernon Valley had hired security guards to keep people attending the concert away from the homes on the mountain.

We arrived home early Sunday evening. Jack opened the front door and entered our house. He found a young man with his girlfriend sleeping in our bedroom! Without hesitation, Jack opened the door and threw the two intruders out the front door. We were horrified and angry. This story comes up often when I have a meeting with Gene. End of this story is that that was the last outdoor concert ever held in the base area at Great Gorge.

A look back at the lasting impact skiing at Vernon Valley had on many of the young skiers who remember it so fondly seems an appropriate end to this chapter. Bonnie Belcher Godfrey, a frequent Vernon Valley/Great Gorge skier from its earliest days, recently wrote a lovely story in which she shares her fond memories of learning to ski at Vernon Valley. Bonnie grew up in Sussex County and now lives in Lake Hopatcong. She is an executive with a large telecommunications company. Here is how she remembers that first skiing experience. This is a nice reminder that there were many enjoyable days of skiing at Vernon Valley over the years.

My First Adventure On Skis

I remember my first adventure on skis like it was yesterday. I was holding on to the Rope Tow at Vernon Valley Ski Resort in northern New Jersey. My skis were older than I was at that point. I remember my mother getting them from a neighbor for free near my home. They had old "Tony the Tiger" stickers still *on them from the last owner. My mother did not want to waste money on new skis; she thought I would lose interest quickly. My ski boots were more like hiking boots with tie laces. My blue-topped wool socks were turned down over my boots and my "Levi" jeans were tucked into them. I wore a hooded sweatshirt over my pajamas. My mother bought me a large, white snowball-hat that was very warm. I prayed no one would see me in that hat.*

The year was 1969. I was five years old. I burned through a bunch of mittens that winter, but surprisingly, not my patience. Hanging on to a heavy rope to the top of a 100-foot hill was, for a little girl, no less adventurous than skiing in the Alps or scuba diving. That's what is so compelling about adventure: It is relative. I remember walking over to the "bunny hill" with my skis that day. As I walked across the base, I watched two teenagers. They were warm and dry, and could turn wherever they wanted to. Watching them was a turning point in my life. Those skiers knew something I didn't know – how to have a good time on top of the snow instead of rolling around in it, as I always did.

I find it strange that I can remember everything about that day more than four decades ago. Over the years, I have asked a lot of people about their first day on skis. If yours was after the age of four, you can probably remember every detail: the clothes you wore, the trails you climbed, or lifts you rode – even how blue the sky was. I can remember the music on the radio that was playing from the Octagon Lodge. I can remember the colors of the chairlifts: brown, red and yellow. When I ask people about their first day on skis, they smile and get a faraway look in their eyes. I believe they remember everything about it because it was their first taste of total freedom. I remember going across "Sugar Slope" at whatever speed my adrenaline would take me. The first time I completed a turn through the fall line, I felt that the entire world had opened up and was now mine.

Before my first day was over, I was finally able to complete about 65 percent of a turn on one side before I crashed or slid down the slope on my stomach, laughing at the top of my lungs. More than 40 years later, I still look forward to my first turn every season with the same anticipation I had when I headed to the snowy foothills of Vernon Valley. Now I spend every winter out west for at least a few weeks exploring Montana, Utah, Colorado, California or Wyoming. Nevertheless, I will never forget 1969 and the "bunny hill" at Vernon Valley.

Vernon Valley continued to operate for a number of years. In 1998 it was announced that Vernon Valley and Great Gorge were to be bought out by Intrawest, a large real estate conglomerate which specialized in ski areas. Several years later, they started construction on a huge ski complex featuring new residential areas. The ski facilities were greatly expanded. Space available in this book is limited to the earlier days of skiing in Vernon Township. The tremendous growth extended to a full fledged golf mecca. At the start of this book, it was announced that the entire Mountain Creek facility had been sold to a new entity. Much is being written about the future plans for the entire valley. Details on these plans are available at the Mountain Creek offices. The future of our little valley however, remains for others to tell.

Jack & Peg skiing

126

Crystal Springs Resort – 2011

– CHAPTER 17 –

NEW ADVENTURES

Wolf Paw

Once Jack was fully recovered from his heart attack, he began to get restless. He had decided that he did not want to return to being in charge of Hidden Valley and was looking for a less stressful career path. The word went out that he was available to do consulting work in the Sussex County area. The first to approach him was George Theobold, who was hoping to turn a project he called Wolf Paw into a quality golf course development.

The Theobold Family owned a large tract of farmland property in Vernon. The property was owned by George Theobold and his brothers, Horace, Calvin and Harry. When George sought Jack out in 1997, he had already engaged a management group which specialized in golf course and golf community development. At that time, the only large golf course in the Vernon area was at the Playboy Hotel. George put Jack on retainer to serve as the liaison between the architects, engineers and golf course designers. As part of his contract, Jack was also to coordinate efforts to receive the necessary local, county and State land use agency approvals for the development.

This was when Jack met the famous Robert von Hagge who George had selected to design their proposed Wolf Paw golf course. Jack was eager to see this famous golf course architect at work, knowing that von Hagge, had designed a number of courses in Mexico and across the United States. His designs were quite dramatic, featuring undulating fairways throughout the course. His courses were very beautiful to look at and photograph, but often demanded careful placement of shots on every hole – guess that is where the term target golf came into play. One needed to be very accurate in selecting approaches to greens and fairways. As the reader will learn later, the course at Crystal Springs was also designed by von Hagge and soon earned the title of "The Toughest Golf Course in New Jersey". Those who play it quickly learn to manage each shot and love the challenge. The Crystal Springs course is not geared for the beginner or intermediate golfer, but low handicappers love it.

Once Wolf Paw was laid out and ready for the needed approvals, it ran into several serious road blocks. One of the Theobalds' neighbors had a lovely country estate and some land he leased out for small farming activities and fine cheese-making to maintain the status of a working farm. This gentleman farmer liked having his privacy and opposed any development in the area of his home, except farming. He roused other farmers in the area urging them to help defeat the golf course project. They argued that if the land were developed as a golf course community, it would be adversely impacted by chemicals and other disturbances caused by new building. Most of their protests, we felt, were exaggerated. Witness the more than six courses that now exist in this county. These courses have been applauded for their contribution to bird and wild life sanctuaries, land management and for using only approved fertilizers.

In 1997, a golf community built around a golf course in a rural area was ahead of its time. Environmentalists and local farmers showed up in force at all the Planning Board meetings. Wolf Paw promised to create a "clean" resort industry, not a manufacturing business environment with smoke stack buildings, but failed to sway the local protestors. The application for the project was defeated.

At the time Wolf Paw failed to receive the needed approvals, farmers were still eking out a living by raising crops and struggling to cover their bills. Subsistence farming continued as the main source of employment in the area, mainly because the lack of public transportation for residents made it extremely difficult to commute to jobs in distant urban areas.

Although the Wolf Paw project was turned down, the Theobolds stayed on to live and work in the area. Their farm continued to grow corn and pumpkins. Son Martin opened a successful farm products stand named Heaven Hill Farms. Each fall, Theobold Farm still has hay rides and pumpkin picking. Throughout the year, their small petting zoo brings school children on class trips.

Momma Jean Theobold reactivated some of the barns and began to raise veal calves. Today the farm is recognized as a source for the top-quality Provimi Veal Products used by the finest restaurants throughout the United States.

The Spa, Minerals Golf, Stonehill and Cobblestone Village

After his rather abrupt retirement from the ski business in 1977, but fully recovered from his heart attack, Jack wanted to get back to work. In addition to the chance to work independently on the Wolf Paw project, he also responded to Gene Mulvihill's timely offer to come to work with him on special projects at Vernon Valley. This was another good opportunity to move on and find a less stressful lifestyle. He accepted the challenge.

Once he began working for Gene, the first large project came along quickly. Gene wanted to build a Spa and Health Club on property located halfway between Vernon Valley and Great Gorge. Jack jumped right in and began working with the engineers and architect planning the site. He started by researching sports clubs in the Metropolitan New York/New Jersey area. Good facilities were in big demand and Sussex County had not yet moved into that type of business.

Gene was the type who wanted excitement, adventure and any kind of unusual innovation he thought would help make The Spa at Great Gorge a success. He wanted action! His idea of action meant insisting that The Spa needed indoor tennis courts, a full-length basketball court, room for ballroom dancing, a running track, a state-of-the-art fitness center and even training facilities for boxers.

A key attraction was to be a pool, not just any old pool, but one totally unique! Gene's idea of a real pool came complete with jumps off cliffs, aquariums, indoor pools that extended outdoors, an outdoor pool which could be used even in the winter, tunnels, wading pools, water fountains for children to run under – you name it, he wanted it. He hired a top pool designer, Roy Scovill. Scovill's forte was designing free form pools with beautiful waterfalls. When it came to the design for The Spa, Scovill was even able to incorporate our wonderful views of the surrounding mountains and the valley.

Another special feature Gene and Jack planned for The Spa was the 5-star restaurant known as Kites. It was built to overlook the fancy pools and distant golf courses, as well as many of the indoor sporting activities taking place below.

Much of the credit for the unique design of The Spa belongs to its architect, Jack Murphy of Montville, New Jersey. One of his innovative ideas was to have the indoor running track ringing the building near its ceiling with windows available so runners or walkers could look down and see basketball, tennis and swimming. This broke the monotony of running around an indoor track. Once complete, The Spa was a world class sports club.

Gene's son, Andy, was given the job of spearheading new construction at a new condominium hotel with dining and banquet areas. Andy felt that the hotel and the ancillary facilities would capitalize on the area's early mining days. The facility was aptly named Minerals.

Concurrent with The Spa, Jack was up and running with the development of a large condominium community now known as Stonehill. The complex is the large group of condominiums located on the hill adjacent to The Spa. Its earliest units sold out quickly, and the community has continued to be successful ever since. Jack even received an award for the fine windows he had installed at Stonehill. By 2010, all of these projects were incorporated into the more extensive four season resort area in conjunction with the ski areas.

Once Vernon Valley and Great Gorge ski areas were merged into one and The Spa was opened, Gene needed to attract more summer visitors to his growing empire. The solution was to launch his Action Park at Vernon Valley. Some of the best-known features of Action Park were an alpine slide, which ran from the top of the mountain to the base area, and a spectacular bungee jump. A host of other exciting facilities included fabulous water slides and a children's water park.

Thousands of visitors arrived daily to enjoy the exciting and daring new Action Park.

With The Spa and its golf course launched, Stonehill's first condos selling well and Action Park drawing increasing numbers, the time was ripe for another special assignment for Jack.

He was delighted to be involved in the design of Cobblestone Village. This Village was to be located across the street from the Action Park area and to feature shopping and an array of food and beverage shops. Once it was built, each shop in the Cobblestone Village was owned and operated by individual tenants. For a few years, our children ran a chocolate cookie shop named Kurly's Sweet Tooth. John and Anna Fitzgerald opened a homemade ice cream shop that featured Belgian waffles filled with the ice cream. The new shops were an instant success and a much-needed place to retool and refresh between more action-packed activities.

Next, Gene encouraged the building of a very special miniature golf course and a new Motor World, complete with race cars, bumper cars and a pond for speed boats. It was pretty wild down there when all these rides were running. One of Gene's final innovations in the Cobblestone Village area was to add a very large Oktoberfest Pavilion. This newest pavilion even had its own micro-brewery. Once it opened, Mulvihill, in full lederhosen attire, was often seen leading marching bands as they paraded around the park. The Oktoberfest Pavilion specialized in German foods and beer served up in the open air pavilion. Many years later, the annual Oktoberfest is still a highlight of the fall season at the four season Resort.

All of these newer facilities were within easy reach of the Vernon Valley Ski Area. By the end of 1998, the resort industry was on a roll in Vernon Township. The extensive expansion in the 1990's in housing, golf and summer attractions now combined to offer recreation for all seasons.

Jack, although far from ready to rest on his laurels, could look with pride at what grew from his latest "new adventures".

Minerals Resort & Spa outdoor pools – 2011

Jack &
John Russian

Jack & Peg's home, locker room, pavillion

John, Uncle Jack & Colleen

– CHAPTER 18 –

CRYSTAL SPRINGS

Crystal Springs Swim and Tennis Club

In 1980, a few years after Jack had recovered sufficiently from his heart attack and had gone back to work for Gene Mulvihill on special projects, he began talking about making plans to retire. Not surprisingly, one day he arrived home and announced that he had found a fabulous piece of property that was sure to become our retirement nest egg. He could hardly wait to show it to me.

The property turned out to be what was known by the locals as the Bodner Quarry. This local landmark was located on Old Quarry Road on the outskirts of town, just off of Route 517 and close to the eastern entrance of what is now Crystal Springs. The property he liked had two abandoned limestone quarries and, adjacent to them, 50 acres of farmland and swampland.

The bigger of the two quarries was known as Quarry Lake and was, depending upon the amount of rainfall, a 35-foot deep spring-fed lake with no intake or outlet. Its best feature was the intense color of its deep blue water, highlighted further when sunlight and breezes added a silvery shimmer to its surface. Gazing from the quarry's edge, looking at the blue, blue water, one felt as though one were visiting the Caribbean. Adjacent to the large Quarry Lake was a smaller "Baby Quarry" lake. It, too, had also once been quarried and now only collected rain water.

Surrounding the two quarry lakes was what was then known as the "Big Spring" swamp. Over time, a small swampland had evolved into a larger one. The springs that flowed outward from our Big Spring swamp eventually made their way to larger streams. Those, in turn, led to the Paulinskill River and joined with the headwaters of the Walkill River at a juncture which is now part of the Lake Mohawk Country Club.

The Big Spring swamp was filled with all kinds of wild flowers and fauna. As we soon discovered, the swamp attracted water fowl and beautiful birds that migrate to build their nests there each summer. Beavers also built nests, leaving their little dams scattered across the swamp. Cranes, ducks, swans and geese were regular summer visitors. We also discovered that, at some point in time, an ancient Indian tribe, most likely the Lenni-Lenape, had lived in the area hundreds of years ago.

That first day when Jack invited me to walk the quarry property, I could see for myself what a remarkable find he had made. He had already begun formulating plans for how to convert this beautiful spot into a Swim and Tennis Club. He envisioned himself running a small business. He also saw us building a small retirement home on the property. He even went as far as to show me an ideal spot to build, one that overlooked the Baby Quarry with its beautiful limestone rocks and walls. I pictured a comfortable home where we would grow old together.

Despite the overwhelming charm of this unique spot, I was a bit skeptical about purchasing such a large piece of property and taking on yet another project. To get me to agree to going into another new venture, Jack dangled the proverbial carrot. Since we would need to borrow money to buy the land and build the new club, Jack had to be at his persuasive best. The pièce de résistance of his sales campaign was the name he had for the venture – P.K.'s Bath and Tennis Club. How could I resist?

After a bit of research, Jack learned that the property we explored that day was owned by Howard and Hildegard Hennington of Greenwich, Connecticut. During the summer months, they used the property for weekend getaways. They had an arrangement with Alex Bodner, a local farmer, which suited them well. Bodner was allowed to farm the part of the property that was suitable for farming in return for keeping an eye on the rest of the property. With Bodner overseeing the Hennington property, kids and others who lived nearby assumed the quarry belonged to Bodner and so it was always called Bodner's Quarry.

Bodner had told the local kids that if they helped pick the corn and did other small jobs at the farm, they could come and swim in the Quarry. Other kids, who did not work for Bodner, would often instead just sneak onto the property at dusk for an evening swim. On warm summer evenings, as many as twenty to thirty trespassers could be counted jumping and swimming to their hearts' content.

We have no written records about the quarry, but have been told that over the years a number of drownings occurred there. One suspects, however, that those who drowned were mostly city people who did not know how to swim and did not realize the dangers of jumping into the deep quarry.

The main quarry had another story attached to it. A friend of mine, who worked for me, as a receptionist and telephone operator at Great Gorge, told me that her son purchased a motorcycle and attempted to try an Evil Knievel jump over the Quarry. Unfortunately, his expectations outstripped his skill. He fell far short of clearing his jump across the quarry. Fortunately, he was rescued and was rushed to the hospital for medical assistance. Surprisingly, the staff was able to put his broken legs back into working order.

Once he won me over to the newest project, Jack contacted the Henningtons and began negotiating to buy the property. We were able to strike a reasonable price and soon became the owners of the Bodner Quarry. I was still a bit skeptical about the Swim and Tennis Club idea in this rural Sussex County area. Would people support membership in a club, much less be willing to join a sophisticated sounding "Bath and Tennis Club"? Would local residents understand since most prefer to take a shower. They were not accustomed to showering in the lockers rooms of a swim club!

The part of the property where Jack wanted the club to be sited was where the quarry had once operated. Now, this section had only remnants from quarry operations. In its heyday, rock was extracted, put into wagons and moved to a railroad. The quarried rock then was moved on to kilns and large ovens which separated the iron ore and the limestone. The limestone was then crushed and used for various purposes, primary of which was for fertilizer that enriched farms throughout the county.

We knew immediately this was a special place, despite the unsightly remains from earlier operations. Who could have guessed, however, that it would eventually become a destination four season resort with golf, skiing and a host of other recreational activities?

In 1980 when we first walked the property, it was just an old abandoned limestone quarry with lots of rock and dust, and some farmland. As soon as we had purchased the property, we started to work to get building permits approved. First we applied to the Hardyston Planning Board for permission to build an entry road off Quarry Road and erect buildings for a swim club, bathhouses, a caretaker's apartment and offices. The small swimming pool, three tennis courts and a pavilion with food service facilities we planned to add later.

Grading for parking lot – soon to be 11th hole

Foreman Jeff Stewart during construction 11th fairway at C

Construction began immediately. Creating a large parking area required lots of bulldozing and moving of rock and dirt. Despite this noisy, messy beginning, we were on our way to building our retirement home base— all the while hoping that after paying off the mortgage and the construction costs, we would not be broke.

Our next obstacle came when we needed permits to clear all the slag heaps and the remaining piles of unsold stone off the site. We soon learned the Planning Board was not in favor of setting up a crusher to break up the slag and truck it out of there. Stone crushing is a very noisy and dirty activity. No one wanted that going on in their neighborhood. We were happy to reassure them we did not plan to begin crushing slag.

Some Board members felt that we were pretending that we were going to build a swim club and really wanted a soil removal permit to mine the stone. All we wanted was to remove the slag and create parking and recreation areas. Until the slag was removed, we would not have sufficient flat land for parking and the tennis courts.

One of the Board members felt that we were going to make millions taking away the slag. We had a better idea. At the same time as we were trying to win approvals from the Hardyston Planning Board, construction crews were at work at the new Hidden Valley Ski Area, building an access road to the top of Hidden Valley. We hoped to get the stone moved out of Crystal Springs and sell it to Hidden Valley at a very low price. In our eyes this was a win-win situation for both Hidden Valley and Crystal Springs.

Board members asked how much money we were going to make from selling the stone. Jack estimated that it would probably be a break-even proposition. When the Planning Board heard we were not going to make a fortune, they quickly passed a resolution allowing the removal of the stone. As long as we did not make a pile of money, they were happy to grant the permits. God forbid that a businessman should make money. Once the permits were granted, the road at Hidden Valley was built to the top of the mountain and Crystal Springs now had flat land on which to build P.K.'s Bath and Tennis Club.

During the first construction phase, we both continued working at our jobs, but also spent many hours supervising P.K.'s Bath and Tennis Club. As an early security move, we hired a night watchman and installed a trailer where he could live. This helped keep trespassers out. No longer was anyone allowed to come in for evening skinny dipping. The first night watchman we hired was Jeff Stewart. Jeff had his hands full that first summer, but he managed to keep things under control.

Humble beginnings at Crystal Springs

Our new Crystal Springs Swim and Tennis Club, then going by its original name of P.K.'s Bath and Tennis Club, opened for the summer season in 1982. To our great disappointment very few people joined P.K.'s Bath and Tennis Club that first year.

Once we closed for the season, we boarded up our buildings for the winter months of 1983. One morning a call from the Hardyston Police came to me at Hidden Valley reporting that our bath houses, offices and cottage had been broken into and set on fire. Since everything was boarded up for the winter, we never expected we needed to insure our vacant buildings.

This became yet another test of our endurance. The damage was extensive. The fire that teenagers had built became so hot that the PVC pipes installed for the water and plumbing systems under the poured concrete floors were melted into the ground. Replacement costs were high. Suddenly, we needed to put all our expansion plans on the back burner.

When the time came to reopen P.K.'s Swim and Tennis Club for its second season, Jack decided that we needed a new name for our retirement jewel. We needed a more inviting name, one that would attract more members. Out went "P.K." In came the more compelling "Crystal Springs", a name that evoked the brilliant quarry waters. By then, I was enjoying their newly discovered treasure. She was willing to give up her promised immortality and have the original name fade into obscurity.

That spring, we sold our Great Gorge chalet and moved to the little apartment at Crystal Springs. We loved living on our 50 acres. Each evening we walked the property until we found a peaceful spot to sit and look at the beautiful blue waters of the quarry. We purchased a female Golden Retriever, who ultimately became our "Chipper Mountain Dog". Chipper was an easy companion, happy at home at Crystal Springs and equally comfortable during working hours at Hidden Valley.

Our evening walks always included Chipper running along beside us. As sad as we were to leave our Great Gorge home on the mountain, we quickly embraced the beauty of living in this very special place at Crystal Springs.

After our first two years at Crystal Springs, however, we realized that we could not generate enough income from the Swim Club to stay afloat, literally and figuratively. We had to come up with fresh ideas to keep our dream solvent. After a bit of brainstorming, two good ideas seemed workable.

The first idea involved picnics. We knew that large companies hosted picnics every year. Companies planned these picnics to give employees and their family members a day of relaxation and fun. In return, they could usually count on some increased good will in employee-employer relations.

Where better to have a company picnic, we strategized, than at Crystal Springs? We already had wonderful swimming to offer. To be competitive, we needed more attractions. We began by building a snack bar, a very large open-air pavilion with a full commercial-sized kitchen, three ball fields and tennis courts. Then we added horseshoe pits, basketball and volley ball courts, and enlarged the parking areas we would need to handle such groups.

Marketing this new facility became our top priority, and the picnic business was a big success. All through the company picnic era, we also continued to operate the pool and tennis courts at the club. To handle increased numbers, we expanded the swimming area to include the northern part of the big quarry. Once our teenaged life guards named that part "North Beach". Everyone who visited, young or old, wanted to spend time there.

North Beach featured small wading pools, a boardwalk, and large sand boxes and wading pools for little kids. We also installed swim docks and a very long diving board. Back then, with a quarry that was 35 feet deep, we had no concerns about people hitting the bottom, nor were we worried about the potential liability of a diving accident.

We learned another valuable lesson once we opened up our facility for corporate picnics. We hired adult seniors to take over the kitchens. Their enthusiasm – whether shucking clams, husking fresh corn, contributing secret recipes for their family's potato salads, cooking sausage or grilling the best large German hot dogs we could buy—was priceless. These master cooks also won accolades for their high-quality hamburgers cooked to order.

Some of our largest outings included Gitano Jeans, the Iron Workers Union and a number of Teamsters organizations. Once the word got out about Crystal Springs' picnic facilities, companies came from all over the New York/New Jersey area. We kept these picnicking weekend warriors active playing softball, basketball, horseshoes and tennis. Company employees and their young families also enjoyed egg relays and sand bag races. Some companies hired professional clowns to keep young children busy throughout the day. One of the companies even rented some elephants for picnickers to ride around the property.

Still, swimming in the beautiful crystal-clear waters of the Quarry was the highlight of the day. Ah, yes. These were definitely the good old days when families had a day of fun at Crystal Springs.

The unusually deep water in the quarries gave us another idea for making some much-needed extra income. Deep waters were a perfect setting for scuba diving. We could use this atypical feature to create a scuba diving business. We opened the quarry as a dive-testing grounds on weekends throughout the spring, summer and fall.

A particularly attractive feature of the new business was the dive platform submerged thirty feet from the water's surface. With such a platform in place, divers could avoid the murky silt below. Silt had been collecting on the quarry floor for many years, but it was no place for practicing new skills.

The quarry was deep enough for beginning divers to practice skills they needed to acquire before they ventured out to more challenging ocean waters or swam among coral reefs. Before long most of the dive schools in the Metropolitan area brought their students to Crystal Springs for certification. The extra revenue we received from the scuba business helped. Like the corporate picnics, it was not enough. We then looked for around for expansion ideas.

Crystal Springs Is Introduced to the Smithsonian Institution

After we sold our Great Gorge house, we moved into a charming apartment attached to one of our three buildings at Crystal Springs. We were now officially residents in Hardyston Township. We had visited some of the mines in the area and attended lectures explaining the various rocks and minerals found in these mines. One of my children owned a black light which, when shown on some stones in the area, gives off very beautiful fluorescent colors. We have been told that 25 stones in the Franklin mines are not found anywhere else in the world! Occasionally, a few rock hounds would stop at our quarry to see what it looked like. One of our visitors was a geologist who was sent to Crystal Springs to collect specimens. We gave him and his assistant permission to climb the large face at our big quarry. From our little kitchen window in the apartment, we could see the glow of their lights at night when they were climbing. They found about ten specimens which they marked, wrapped and secured in their truck. They then delivered our stones to the Smithsonian. When we visited there, we looked but never could find our samples. There were thousands of specimens of all kinds of stones that are stored and catalogued there. If you want to see a famous fluorescent Franklinite rock with a light shining on it, you would enjoy going to the Franklin Mineral Museum.

Crystal Springs Golf and Residential Community Takes Over

Jack was a fine golfer. Like many men, he dreamed of building his own golf course some day. Now we were living in a place where this might be possible. Returning to his usual treasured maps, he laid out a plan for a new residential and golf course community with an 18-hole golf course. Of course, we Kurlanders did not have the funds or the skills to develop a facility of this magnitude. So, Jack assembled a small group of investors to put in the funds needed to purchase options on the properties he felt would be necessary to build the golf course and residential community he was planning.

Our longstanding friend, Fred Lange, was the first to see this as an acceptable opportunity. Fred was already well acquainted with our little Swim and Tennis Club. He loved to play tennis and hang around the club. He spent countless days chatting with members and eating lots of hot dogs and barbeque chicken.

Shortly afterward, Dennis Mamchur, Greg Wright and a few others who purchased stock in a new company, now named Big Spring Development. Their funds gave Jack the purchasing power he needed to move ahead. Jack then assembled enough additional land to accommodate a planned residential community.

Always the consummate salesman, Jack approached many of the New Jersey builders who had expressed an interest in purchasing part or all of Crystal Springs. Our long-standing friend, Joe Riggs, turned out to have the most appealing offer of the lot.

Joe was a partner in the Bowling Green Golf Course in Jefferson. He knew the golf business and was an experienced builder of homes and condominiums in North Jersey.

We knew the Riggs family very well. Joe had been best man at our daughter's wedding to Dean Peters. He already ran a successful medium-sized home-building business and was anxious to cut his teeth on a much bigger project. Jack's plans were also, in turn, very appealing to Joe. The real estate market was booming, and new home construction was growing by leaps and bounds. This seemed like a wonderful opportunity for both parties.

Jack and Joe Riggs reached an agreement. Joe's company, Swedeland Forge, purchased our property and started work to obtain the approvals needed to build this new community. Swedeland made a substantial down payment. We took back a sizable first mortgage. It was to be paid back over a 20-year period with funds that the developer would generate from the golf course and the real estate development. We thought that our future was secure and that our retirement years would be idyllic.

We hired Robert von Hagge, the well-known golf course architect, to design Crystal Springs Golf Course. At the same time, Swedeland Forge was at work designing and building the residential component of the Crystal Springs golf and residential community. The first roads were built and several single-family homes were constructed in the Tannery Hill section of the community.

The company also started building the Cedars condominium neighborhood, townhomes, in the Sugar Maple Lane neighborhood and other large single-family homes in the Oaks section.

From the first, real estate sales did not grow as expected. Hundreds of people came every week to see this wonderful new development. Few bought. Swedeland set high standards of architectural style and landscaping designs, and the new homes were built to high quality standards. Still sales remained slow.

The commitment of money to accomplish the selling of these properties was tremendous. Because sales were not as projected, before long Swedeland could not afford to continue building. The money was running out. The Swedeland project had been financed by Carteret Savings Bank. The Carteret Savings Bank was under pressure to meet its obligations. With no returns coming in from the Swedeland project at Crystal Springs, the Resolution Trust Company (R.T.C), an arm of the Federal Government, moved in and forced Carteret Savings into bankruptcy. Swedeland was also then forced into a Chapter 11 form of bankruptcy. Chapter 11 typically allows the debtor time to try to get commitments of funds from qualified investors.

The Resolution Trust moved instead to mandate that the whole project be sold at public auction. This now became the perfect storm. Little hope remained for salvaging the golf and housing project. The mortgage we held on the Crystal Springs property went south.

We decided that we needed to find jobs and go back to work once again. That was quite a jolt. We sold every piece of property we owned, including our Tannery Hill home and a nice condominium we owned in Tequesta, Florida.

Once the dust settled, we bought an eighty-year-old farm house near the entrance to Crystal Springs on Route 94 and moved in on Mother's Day. The house needed much repair and decorating. On the other hand, it had two acres, beautiful gardens and the potential to be a very charming home.

I took a job at Crystal Springs, trying to generate sales for the Swedeland homes. Selling properties from a company which was in reorganization as permitted by the bankruptcy laws was very difficult. The party was over.

Today people tell me their tales of woe about the losses they incurred when their homes fell 20% to 30% in value, or they were unable to sell their home at the price they had paid five years before. I often want to say to them,

"Let me tell you about MY real estate losses." They should read this book. Our Crystal Springs story will make them feel better when it comes to comparing their losses with those we incurred.

As a final comment on what came next – Swedeland Forge attempted to obtain the chance to reorganize their company and be allowed to continue to build and sell at Crystal Springs. I have been told by reliable sources that they had a bank and some investors lined up to resume the project. The Resolution Trust ruled that it was too little too late. Their plan was not acceptable. The property was to be sold at public auction.

The rest of this story is a matter of record. At the time of the auction, Gene Mulvihill lined up an investor group which, at the Public Auction, put in the highest bid for the property, becoming the new owners of all of Crystal Springs.

Swedeland Forge Company still builds homes in New Jersey. Joe Riggs is a Vice President with K. Hovnanian, one of New Jersey's largest builders, and the Riggs family still owns and operates Bowling Green Golf Course in Jefferson, New Jersey.

The golf course at Crystal was completed. As local lore goes, currently a group of senior male members at Crystal Springs have formed a club named

Old 10th at Crystal Springs

the ABC's. When they make a reservation at one of the courses now associated with the Resort, they plead ABC, "Anything but Crystal." This course is just too tough for them. Fortunately they now have a choice of five other courses - Ballyowen, Wild Turkey, Black Bear, Great Gorge Country Club (the former Playboy Legends Course), and Grand Cascades. The Crystal Springs course has earned the distinction of being the toughest course in New Jersey. I think it might be among the toughest in the world.

– CHAPTER 19 –

BLACK BEAR

By the early 1990's that what he needed most his four seasons resort was to Gene Mulvihill could see to round out his concept of have more golf. The first two golf courses opened in the area were the nine-hole executive course built at Minerals in the late 1970's and the 27-hole Legends Golf Course built in 1972 as part of Hugh Heffner's Playboy Club Hotel complex. As we learned in the last chapter, in 1992 the challenging new course at Crystal Springs had opened under the capable management of the Swedeland Forge Development Group. By now, in the early 1990's, the whole area had become a Mecca for year-round recreation, but its golf courses were still unable to keep up with demand.

Sensing the need for even more tee times, Gene asked Jack to find a property for the construction of an 18-hole championship golf course. Gene wanted badly to extend his enterprises and become a presence in the golf business. His main criterion was that Jack should find a site upon which to build a new course that was within a five-mile radius of the existing ski areas and the other recreation facilities he had already developed in Vernon.

After his study of geodetic maps and tax maps, Jack settled on a former dairy farm in Franklin Borough. For many years the Fasalo family had successfully operated their well-known Fasalo Dairy. With the coming of age of another generation, the family had run out of interested family members, and they proved anxious to sell. The property had all the right features including water, good drainage, accessibility to a major road and approximately 300 acres of suitable terrain. The Fasalo Dairy filled the bill.

Contracts were signed, approvals were obtained and Jack went to work on another new golf course for Sussex County. He envisioned that this new course would be held to the standards of the Sussex County Golf Preserve whose mission statement he had helped formulate in 1992. In 1993, Carl Waldenmaier was appointed to the office of Director of the Preserve located at the Black Bear Golf Course. His specific job at Black Bear was to oversee and enforce the new Preserve standards. These standards required that new courses be environmentally friendly, preserving wetlands and the natural habitat. This meant any 18-hole course built in the county must preserve the wetlands and the natural habitat of existing animals, birds and water fowl. By working so diligently to follow Preserve standards at Black Bear, Jack hoped that all future golf course development in Sussex County would also meet Preserve standards.

John Kurlander – Early Manager at Black Bear

Once his design was approved, Jack was given the go-ahead from Gene to build the course. Gene was to raise the money while Jack was to oversee the construction and all aspects of the new course. For his efforts, Jack agreed to take 25% ownership of this new golf course. The course itself stretched across hills and valleys that dipped from the Hamburg Mountain range. It offered beautiful vistas and distant views of varied terrain – all within a very few feet from busy Route 23. Part of the land was in Franklin and part was in Hardyston. This meant obtaining approvals from both towns, in addition to meeting county and state regulations. Although he had never before designed his own course, Jack successfully overcame the problem issues that came up with wet lands, streams, drainage and design.

After the property was purchased, Jack invited me to hike the property with him so he could show me what he planned. Walking with him was inspiring. I listened to him point out where everything would be situated – from driving range, to club house, to exciting golf holes and on from a valley in the back nine to various stream crossings and water holes. He could see them all and knew exactly where each piece would fit. He could see the whole layout in his mind – a gift he had that few others possessed.

Richard Downes is a Sparta, New Jersey attorney who was instrumental in writing the New Jersey Land Use Act. All developers must adhere to this act when building or constructing a project in the State of New Jersey. As one of the authors of this act, Downes could appreciate Jack's talent for envisioning what would work where. This is how he expressed Jack's gift:

"Jack Kurlander was like Mozart who heard the music in his head and then went to the manuscript to memorialize his music, music which still exists after 200 years. Jack could see the ski areas and the golf courses before they were put on formal plans and maps which evolved into his complexes. Hopefully they too will stand the test of time."

While hiking that day, we noted no-trespassing signs posted throughout the property. The signs said that the land was to be used exclusively for the Black Bear Rod and Gun Club. Immediately we both agreed. The perfect name for the course would be Black Bear.

Today, golfers at Black Bear are sometimes treated to the sight of a lovely black momma bear instructing her cubs on how to climb trees and find food. Visits by the native black bears here are largely unexpected and add a bit extra to the typical golfing day. Of course, golfers are cautioned about going near the bears, especially if momma bear has two or three cubs with her. She is very protective of her little ones. Our bears at Black Bear sometimes also enjoy evening visits to the Dunkin Donuts store that sits on the edge of the Black Bear property. After a season of sampling the store's castoff high-caloric treats, our bears become rather fat. Word has it that they prefer the sugar donuts over the whole wheat donuts.

Since the 1970's, the bear population in Sussex County has struggled to survive in a habitat overrun by the rapid growth of new housing developments. The State of New Jersey has even permitted legal bear hunts to control the bear population living in the northern parts of the state. Too many bears threaten the availability of food found in the woods and on the mountains. This forces bears to infringe upon residential communities. Residents are cautioned about the futility of thinking that bear-proof garbage cans will stop bears from foraging for food in residential areas. Some people are even foolish enough to put food out on their properties. This creates a further nuisance. We might add our thoughts that the same caveat is needed when it comes to feeding deer. The deer population is all but out of control now. These once-desired forest friends now destroy gardens and farms, and are a costly nuisance.

From the beginning, Jack's design for Black Bear was aimed at having it as "user friendly". He wanted to distinguish it from the very demanding course at Crystal Springs, which had been rated the Toughest Course in the State of NJ. A difficult course that appeals primarily to the more advanced golfer has little appeal for the older golfer or to the beginner or novice golfer. The Crystal course requires accuracy and ability to overcome the many challenges of the course.

Dozer Dave & Jack shape new layout at BB

When Jack was building the course, I gave him a mandate. He must make Black Bear a welcome place for women. For too many years, women had been treated as second class members at most country clubs. I insisted that Black Bear should offer a way for women to reach the greens reasonably close to the number for par. Less athletic women should still be able to enjoy their golf without needing the build or the strength to play 6,000 yard courses in regulation.

Thanks to Jack, women golfers can regularly be seen at Black Bear enjoying their own foursomes as well as playing with spouses or male friends. In June 2011, a member of one of the Ladies Golf Leagues even hit a hole in one when playing the celebrated par-three 7th water hole. Locally, this hole is known as Jack's Crossing – so named for the many balls Jack donated to the golf gods on his first shot. It remains a challenging hole. Most memorable is the lovely Jack Kurlander Memorial Garden, which was planted with a full view of Jack's favorite hole, the challenging 7th. Readers are invited to stop by to see the plaque on their way to the 8th hole.

When the news went out that Jack was building a new course, several architects contacted him wanting to design the course. One day we found a message on our answering machine at home. Bob von Hagge was calling from Mexico. He shouted something like, "Kurlander you had better have me there to design that blankety, blank course of yours." I heard and said in response, "Jack already has laid out a very fine course. Thanks anyway." Von Hagge and other famous course designers tried to win the design contract. This time, Jack was ready to branch out on his own.

Once Jack completed his design, he used local contractors as much as possible to build to his design specifications. Black Bear employed some very talented "shapers" who knew how to turn the bulldozer into a sculptor's tool. They made mounds and fairways pleasant to the eye, which in turn added enjoyment for the golfer. Jack was especially fortunate to have Richard LeBar join the construction crew and serve as Black Bear's first Greens Keeper.

Richard LaBar – Early days at Crystal Springs Swim & Tennis Club

LeBar had first worked for us in 1982 when we owned and operated the Crystal Springs Swim and Tennis Club. Back then, he had proved his worth while still a teenager as someone able to super-vise our summer employees – most of whom, like Richard himself, were high school students. As a teenager, Richard had looked up to Jack, and Jack in turn quietly became Richard's surrogate father. Now, in 1994, Richard had a degree from Rutgers with a major in Agronomy and Golf Course Man-agement. Jack was happy to hire him once more. This time around as they worked together to build the new course, Richard worked with him daily on a more equal basis for the two years it took to get the new course built.

Construction money to build the course was always a challenge. Jack and John Steinbach often used their own funds to cover the delivery of pipe, fertil-izer, seed or construction equipment. In addition to everything else he did to help, John Steinbach planned for and planted the trees on the course to separate parallel holes. The trees thrived. Today they add to the beauty and character of the course.

Jack had the forsight when it came to making plans, to acquire a liquor license. This would enable a club to plan many functions at the golf course. Golf courses are popular for catering weddings and for golf tournaments. He knew Black Bear would need to obtain a liquor license. As soon as one be-came available, he used personal funds to purchase a license, rather than wait to find new investors who could put up more capital.

Early on, another key hire Jack made was to have the well-known David Glenz open a golf school at Black Bear. His school thrived, and it gave additional credibility to the course reputation. Glenz was also a big help to Jack by offering some very fine advice throughout our design and construction phase. The author particularly liked what David suggested for shaping the par-five 12th Hole. We all had hoped that there would be a waterfall installed there someday. When water demands for the course were needed more elsewhere, David came up with ideas to add rock formations as eye-catching as a waterfall might have been.

During the construction phase, Jack wakened early every day and headed to the Black Bear site. He set up an office in a small and shabby green house located on Route 23 in Franklin. The local historical society indicates this house was most likely the farm house that had once been the original farm house for the Fasalo Farm. Rose Fasalo, the matriarch of the family, died a few years ago. Since none of her heirs are available to substantiate that Jack's first office was once her home, no one is certain. What locals left in the area do remember, however, is that Rose was a tough old lady who knew how to drive a hard bargain. Most likely Jack's acquisition of the Fasalo Farm was a hard-won bargain for both.

In the days when Black Bear was under construction, the crew sometimes talked about a cave they had heard was under the golf course near the valley holes on the back nine. Jack hoped that whatever had hallowed out this cave might be the answer to solving the problem of having an adequate supply of water available on the property to keep the greens and fairways watered. Golfers today can appreciate how essential that valley is in trapping sufficient water to maintain the golf course. The visible clues as one looks at the valley are the number of sinkholes created by the limestone that lies under the earth in that area. Every sinkhole depression indicates a place where water most probably has collected.

Some of the sinkholes visible on the back nine had small openings, just large enough to enable someone to crawl under the ground and verify a source of water. When asked, some of the crew volunteered to go into what turned out to be an entrance to a cave. Joe Tanis is now Pro Shop Manager at Crystal Springs. At the time Black Bear was under construction, however, Joe had recently finished college and had been hired to work on the construction crew.

Joe and his brother put on safety harnesses and vests and quietly entered the cave, crawling on their bellies. They explored a little but opted to go in only a short distance. Proceeding farther was not safe since no one knew what they might find – snakes, rabbits or cadavers of unknown heritage. Of course, their intent in exploring was to find a useful water source. To their disappointment, they did not go far enough to see that water draining from the valley on the back nine, rather than collecting as a useful source of water, went instead into the limestone and its sinkholes.

To digress a bit – most believe that one can trace all this water down into the well-known aquifer that lies beneath land running from Franklin to the Black Earth district surrounding Pine Island, New York. My understanding is that the water which flows from these aquifers north to the Wallkill River continues to flow up to a point just south of Albany. Eventually, this water then finds its way south again and flows on to the Atlantic Ocean. I am told that the Wallkill is one of a very few rivers in North America which flows north. Driving south recently from Burlington, Vermont, to New York State I noted that the Wallkill River flows through the farmlands under more than seven bridges. A careful observer can spot all seven on the road through Orange County that travels beside the river and eventually ends in northwest New Jersey at the river's home source in Hardyston. That's your geography lesson for the day. If you are at a cocktail party some night and cannot think of an interesting topic to bring up, you can say, "And by the way, did you know that very few rivers in the United States flow north?" Next time you are on the New York Throughway, watch for the signs for the Wallkill River on your right and left reflecting where the Walkill waters are travelling.

Black Bear Golf Course opened in July of 1996 to wide acclaim. Ever since then, it has always been particularly popular as a recreational course for amateur golfers, especially since it is known as the least expensive of the six courses that now make up the Crystal Springs Resort. The par 72 course offers 6,652 yards of golf with water in play on three holes. It also has some interesting bits of history that make it unique.

When I played the 7th hole, I often noted that on the left side of the green there was a tree with the handle from an old truck sticking out of it. I was always intrigued and could not imagine how that could have happened. When looking for the handle recently, I noted it was missing. I doubt that the tree grew so high that the truck handle would now be out of sight. I am tempted to find another handle and have it installed as a replacement. For now its disappearance seems to be just another mysterious, unexplained part of Black Bear's history.

On the first day Black Bear opened, we had a man named George work as our first starter. George still works there today and has seen just about everything at Black Bear. Recently, he mentioned that he, too, was looking for the old truck handle he used to see emerging out of the tree. Neither George nor I have been able to find that handle any more. We continue to watch for signs of where it has gone. Even more intriguing, George did tell me about a spot near the 7th green where concentrated rays of sun light often beam in late in the evening. He surmises that this was the spot where the Lenni Lenape Indians, attracted by the rather mysterious phenomena of unusual light, held their evening powwows.

The original Indians had hallowed grounds here and so it remains. In 2006 the Kurlander family held a private memorial service to dedicate the spot near the 7th hole where the Jack Kurlander Memorial Garden is located. The family gathered there to sprinkle Jack's cremains into the pond that lies beside the 7th hole. The grandchildren participated and commented that Opa loved that spot. How nice to know that this is the source of the water supply for the entire golf course. Now Jack's ashes are everywhere through the course watering system. When you hit a good shot anywhere on the course, I hope you will say "Thank You, Jack!" I do. I like to think that maybe he is watching up there, somewhere rooting for us to make that good shot.

The famous 7th at Black Bear

– CHAPTER 20 –

BALLYOWEN: JACK'S GREATEST FIND

While driving around Sussex County, Jack was always looking at mountains and dreaming of new ski slopes. If he saw a mountain he liked, he would purchase a geodetic map and begin checking the mountain's special characteristics including exposure, vertical drop, streams and nearby rivers. After retiring from the ski business, his thoughts turned instead to finding land with golf course potential. Like a kid in a candy shop, he would hike or drive to the boundaries of surveyed properties that he perceived might be suitable land for a golf course. Just as he had earlier with ski slopes, again, if the land seemed promising, his enthusiasm would bubble, the map study would begin and he would start looking for ways to make it happen.

One afternoon in December of 1997, Jack arrived home early. It was obvious that he had found another golf course property. "Get in the Jeep," he shouted. "I want to show you the most astounding piece of land I have ever seen." Off we went to Wheatsworth Road in Hamburg, New Jersey, a street name recognizable to many for its Americana history.

This historic country road was once the site of a flourishing flour mill built in 1808. Eventually, the mill began turning out branded crackers as the key part of its operations. Later, the mill and its operations were taken over by the Plastoid Corporation and converted to the manufacture of wire and cable. In 1930, Plastoid built its famous castle as an attachment to its factory. For a bit of whimsy, the company decided to open up their castle as an amusement attraction known as the Gingerbread Castle. Since then, the Castle has had several lives from Halloween haunted house to restaurant, to its latest status as an historic landmark.

The first thing Jack and I saw that day, turning off Route 23 onto Wheatsworth Road, were beautiful stone pillars. These large pillars were built of native stone and trimmed with tiles replicating the famous Wheatsworth crackers and cookies that were once produced in the now abandoned factory. Those same pillars also once marked the gateway turn for the more famous Gingerbread Castle.

In their younger days, our children enjoyed their trips to the Castle. Teenagers dressed in character costumes greeted visitors to the Castle and told stories as they guided you up the steep steps to the top of the Castle. Once there, guests were met by witches tending their cauldrons of steamy "poisonous" brew. These young docents also enchanted visitors with their tales of Humpty Dumpty, Jack and Jill, and the Wicked Witch of the West or captured their attention by hinting at the mysterious doings of the Castle's current residents. To be chosen for these jobs was quite an honor. The original Gingerbread Castle closed during the Great Depression, never on subsequent revivals to regain its earlier magic. Those of us who enjoyed the castle in its heyday, however, like to think of it as one of Walt Disney's inspirations for the many movies and theme parks he brought to the young children of America.

On the particular day of this story we continued another mile down Wheatsworth Road and soon saw an old gravel road jutting off to the south. We drove down the gravel road until we were stopped by a chain-link fence. The fence was padlocked and full of warning signs about trespassing. Not deterred, we found a way around the fence and, bothered only by a few grazing sheep, drove on up the hill. This proved to be the site of an abandoned sand and gravel quarry operation. The quarry had originally been owned by a well-known English company. After so many new developers moved into Sussex County and needed its building materials, the usable sand and gravel had been exhausted. All suitable building ingredients had long since been stripped off the land. Now, as far as the eye could see, what remained were only reclaimed pastures full of sand and rocks.

"This is just the way things look in Ireland and Scotland," Jack assured me. "All their wonderful world-famous golf courses have land that looks just like this. Most of them were built in the early 1900's when it was not unusual to see goats and sheep grazing on and around the courses. They just dug a few bunkers to add more challenge to the game."

Our Jeep ride was a bumpy one. I hung on, hoping that the Jeep would not break down in the middle of 300 acres of very isolated property. Jack continued in his tour guide fashion. He pointed out where he envisioned the future ponds and fairways would be and where the clubhouse would sit, a spot at the highest point on the property and one that enjoyed a panoramic view in all directions. As we found out later, this summit location is also ideal for viewing some sensational sunsets. Jack especially loved the location for the back nine. The aura of this magnificent piece of Sussex County land comes complete with undulating land, natural outcroppings of limestone and replicas of what appear to be Indian etchings sketched on several sections of beautiful white stone.

The evening of our Jeep ride we attended the company's annual Christmas Party, which that year was being held at Black Bear. Jack impatiently awaited the arrival of Gene Mulvihill. He quickly escorted him to our table and began to describe what he had seen. One of Jack's jobs with the company was to find land suitable for golf course development and then arrange for its purchase at the best price possible. This course would enhance the fledgling four season resort complex Gene and his company planned for the area. Amazingly, the site of this miracle was less than five miles from the existing Crystal Springs and the Black Bear Golf Courses.

Jack told Gene he thought that the new course should be called Ballybunion USA as a tribute to Ireland's world famous course. It was never named Ballybunion USA, but instead was replaced by the choice of Ballyowen for its name. "Owen" is an Irish derivative of the name "Eugene". Its choice was a subtle salute to Gene for having the foresight to build this course. On closer look, one can also spot a Gene-like replica if you examine the course logos closely.

After that night, Gene went into high gear and put together an investor group to fund this soon-to-be top golf course. He did not care about the cost. He wanted the finest. Of course, in the spirit of friendly rivalry, Gene also wanted to build his own top-flight course, one that would match or better the one owned by his long-time friend Bob Brennan. Bob had built the central New Jersey course, Due Process Stable – a name borrowed from the active interest in horseracing that exists in that same Colts Neck section of New Jersey. I have been told that The Due Process Stable membership fee is so upscale that if you want to be accepted as a member and you ask what the costs are, the applicant is automatically rejected. We might also add here that although Brennan is no longer involved in the golf business, the two remain close friends.

Much credit for the rather immediate success of the unique Ballyowen course can be attributed to course designer Roger Rulewich. Rulewich had become famous as the Robert Trent Jones point man in the field before he went on to form Rulewich and Fleury in the mid 1990's. Here at Ballyowen, Rulewich was commissioned to apply his expertise to the course routing, design and construction. The result was spectacular.

All the staff members who contributed ideas for Ballyowen's unique elegance also deserve credit. No doubt, Julie Mulvihill had a lot to add when it came to choosing uniforms and dress codes. The kilts on many staff members, the short skirts on the food and beverage servers, the dress codes for Pro Shop and Cart Yard staff all have a common theme that seem to reflect Julie's hand at work behind the scenes. One of the nicest attractions of all is the bagpiper and his music. Over the years, he has repeatedly charmed guests with the lilting music he plays most evenings around 5:00 or 6:00pm, often as the sun is setting in the west. He takes his stance a distance away from the clubhouse between the 17th and 18th holes and pipes his salute to the end of another enchanting day at Ballyowen.

Ever since opening day in June of 1998, the course has been noted for its firsts. After the first year of operation, the Ballyowen course was named the #1 Public Golf Course in New Jersey by all of the leading golf publications. Since then, it continues to be chosen as one of the top three. Ballyowen also boasts of being the first public course in New Jersey to offer a caddy program. This has been a huge success and remains available by reservation.

From the beginning, the links-style layout of the course with its wide fairways was so unusual and distinctive that it attracted a very large following of golfers happy to come long distances to northern New Jersey just to enjoy a unique golfing experience. Perhaps the best way to explain how very special Ballyowen has become is to look again at excerpts from the following article. This is how the late Red Hoffman, New Jersey's famous sports writer, explained it in his column of July 5, 1998 for readers of the Sunday Star Ledger:

Not A Tree To Be Seen As New Course Opens

The new Ballyowen Golf Club in Hamburg, which formally opened for public links golfers last Wednesday, may be the most unusual golf course ever built in New Jersey.

Viewed from its traditional-styled clubhouse on its highest point, all but two of its holes can be seen in a panoramic sweep that offers the viewer a scene of unblemished grass punctuated by 75 bunkers and two lakes. The overview is that of a gigantic bowl with a multiplicity of corridors where the playing requirement wind their way in every direction of the compass. It is a beautiful scene, remarkable in the fact that there isn't a tree to be seen. Such a deficiency is characteristic of Oceanside links.

A strip-mining operation is the reason for the Hamburg treeless scene. Ballyowen emerged from the remains of a depleted gravel quarry that left the 233 acre tract devoid of all growth and rife with pits, crevices and scars of the more than 20 tears of excavating that had taken place. What was left was a pitifully sorry expanse of ground that, except for weeds and the like, offered little hope for a productive future.

Jack Kurlander didn't think so. The visionary responsible for converting Sussex County into a ski Mecca when he opened Great Gorge in 1965, he saw the former gravel pit as a future golf course. So did Roger Rulewich. In the last three years he has been building golf courses on his own after 35 years as the chief golf course designer for Robert Trent Jones.

The two visionaries got an early and unexpected bonus. That was when they discovered an unlimited supply of top soil and sand piled around the perimeter of the former excavation operation. When Rulewich told Kurlander, "This is all we need to build a golf course." The earth-moving ultimately more than a quarter million cubic yards, got underway.

The topsoil had been scraped away to get the gravel and the sand "finds" washed from the excavated gravel.

The course was built by the Golf Group of Bernardston, Mass., a cadre of golf course construction experts and artistic shapers who formerly had worked for Jones, usually under the direction of Rulewich.

Ballyowen, from its multiple serpentine teeing areas, can be played from 6,006 to 7,032 yards for the men and from 4,903 yards for the women. Par from any station is 36-36 -72 and the nines are returning.

A six acre lake is a water hazard on the short sixth hole and a lateral hazard on the fifth and seventh, a par-5 and a par-4. A two acre lake has to be carried on the 11th and 15th both one shooters. Each nine finishes below the clubhouse with stout, downhill-then-uphill, par-4 assignments. The 8,000 square-foot 18th green, 50 yards from its frontal tongue to its rear deck, is the biggest on the course.

The course was named with a bow to Ballybunion, the world renowned links in Count Kerry, Ireland. Actually it more resembles Rosses Point in Sligo, a lesser known links on the Emerald Isle.

Ballyowen is the latest of the upscale privately-owned public courses that have proliferated during the last five years in New Jersey. Its green fees are $75 daily and $100 on weekends and holidays, ends and holidays, which include a golf cart and unlimited balls on the practice range. It is situated off Route 23 via Wheatsworth Road, a mile past the famed Gingerbread Castle in Hamburg.

Once the Grand Opening and ribbon cutting and photo ops were over, other promotions were held to jump start the season. The first event was the Toyota Skills Event, an idea conceived by John Kurlander. To preserve the freshly seeded turf still laying down permanent roots, mats for the competitors were laid on top of the first tee area. Then a skills competition took place. Golfers battled for the title of Longest Drive, Closest to the Pin and a few other lesser choices.

The next year, John introduced an ever bigger charity event dubbed the Iron Man of Golf. Many celebrities participated, including several members of the New York Giants football team. The event started at 6:00am. The competitors had to play three complete 18 holes of golf on a schedule that included Black Bear, Crystal Springs and Ballyowen. Jack and John and many of their golfing buddies also played. I played the second year of the event– mostly just for bragging rights and a chance to mingle with a few celebrities up close. My partners that day included Diane Warll and Suzanne Palmer. We started in the fog on the par-3 14th hole at Crystal Springs. We finished at 9:00pm on the 10th hole at Black Bear. Course staff provided box lunches and beverages throughout the day. The staff at each course also worked hard to keep the players moving. The end result was a good time had by all. After the competition was over, we all enjoyed a huge barbeque in the Ballyowen Pavilion. As an added plus, we three local friends managed to get signatures from all the Giants who returned that year. I will not share my scores with the readers, but I have never been sorry that I played in the event and I still proudly display my certificate of completion on my home office wall. My other takeaway from that day was Suzanne, gasping for air, but hitting a great tee shot on the first par-3, 11th hole at Black Bear and then going on to birdie the hole. What a gal.

Roger Rulewich, Ballyowen's course designer, sometimes takes time off from work to visit the Old Course at Ballybunion to study what has made it so outstanding and why this old golf course, built in 1893, has needed few, if any, modifications since then. He always returns with new stories. One he tells is about Tom Simpson and the story that circulates in Ireland about Tom's working days.

One year in the late 1960's Tom Simpson was hired to prepare the Old Course at Ballybunion for the Irish Amateur Closed Championship. The eccentric Simpson always arrived for work in a chauffeur-driven Rolls Royce, accompanied by his glamorous wife, Molly Gourlas. When the time came for lunch each day, Molly could be seen emerging from the car dressed in a flowing cloak and beret and wielding a braided leather riding crop. The Simpsons then proceeded to picnic leisurely on one or the other of the choicest spots to be found on the course. While they languidly emptied the contents of a giant Fornum & Mason's wicker basket, their white-gloved chauffeur stood by polishing the Rolls. Such working pleasure! "If sheer pleasure is the yardstick, then Ballybunion's Old Course gets my vote as the No. 1 in the world," so says Peter Dobereiner, the famous English golf writer. This same superlative is always repeated each time Roger returns home and talks about Ballybunion.

Our story of Ballyowen ends here with a report on the sheep that have grazed on its fenced rough on the back nine for many years. Rumor has it that they came with the property and they did not really belong to anyone. Further investigation reveals that they were not indigenous to the site. Once the greens and fairways were planted and began growing, arrangements were made for some twelve to fifteen sheep, previously raised on a local farm, to be shipped over to begin grazing on the rough that runs long the 12th hole. Water tubs were set up for their drinking water, and they soon settled into their regular routine – eating, sleeping and bleating. Sometimes they hid from the golfers, but eventually they were not bothered by golf balls whizzing past them. Golfers trying to retrieve balls lost in the rough on that side of the hole are the ones who most often reported spotting the grazing sheep. Other golfers even climbed the fence for a short visit with the sheep while searching for their out-of-bounds balls. This is not allowed and is an extra 3 point penalty when reported – which is seldom.

Each year in the thirteen years since Ballyowen opened to the public, one or two more sheep were reported as missing until, as of this writing, the flock has been reduced to one sole survivor. He walks around looking rather lonely. Some of the sheep, we think, disappeared as a result of coyote visits. Others escaped from beneath the wire fencing or fell prey to unknown predators. Their ultimate fate remains a bit of local mystery. The sole survivor is named Diablo, for reasons also unknown. We and the other sheep lovers hope that Ballyowen finds more lambs soon, so Diablo need no longer be the lone grazer. He and the other sheep that once grazed with him lent so much authentic charm to the highland nature of this golfing treasure.

– CONCLUSION –

SUSSEX COUNTY'S MOUNTAIN MEN

During America's pioneer days, leaders emerged to excite our nation with their ideas for building this country. Some of their ideas for expansion were beneficial, others less so. On the positive side, we Americans of today have inherited the benefits of the exploration and invention earlier leaders undertook. At the same time, their legacy has permitted us to preserve our rich natural resources and beautiful landscapes. Sadly, some of the pioneers of the past two centuries gained fame and acclaim as Jesse James-type exploiters who sought only to better themselves by getting rich at the expense of the others they trampled in the process.

Closer to home and closer to our more recent days, large numbers of skiers, golfers and developers arrived in our little valley looking to create and expand the recreational potential of our rural area. Among them, two visionary leaders, Jack Kurlander and Gene Mulvihill, were the first to understand that the best way to preserve the land in Sussex County as a recreational paradise was to set aside tracts of land to be enjoyed by everyone who came to this beautiful place in northern New Jersey.

Jack Kurlander came first. His early dreams were of building a major ski area and later of adding a top-flight golf course for all who would come to enjoy these delights. In early 1963, he began his quest to make those dreams a reality. He built his first major ski area in 1965. Ten years later he started on his path to build his first golf course. During his forty plus years here, he also managed to add to the mix his other love, top-flight tennis, in the form of courts he helped build at Crystal Springs, Hidden Valley, the Playboy Club and The Spa.

I hope you have enjoyed reading my story which gives you a look from inside of how the current four season resort industry in Sussex County, New Jersey blossomed and grew. The book attempts to record the ups and downs of this phenomenal growth – growth which could have only come about through the leadership of the two pioneers who led the way – Jack Kurlander and Gene Mulvihill. The two men were friends and competitors for over thirty-five years. What Jack began, Gene continued and expanded.

Thank you for your interest in and enjoyment of this book. I hope you will share the story with your family, your children and your friends.

– Peg Kurlander

Sussex County's Mountain Men...

Jack Kurlander   **Gene Mulvihill**

– MEMORY LANE –

There are so many things that I want to include in The Tow And I. Many have already been included in earlier chapters. A few stories told by people who knew Jack best are added here in our Memory Lane.

Part of the Eulogy given at Jack's Funeral Mass by Father Jack Boland, Pastor at St. Frances de Sales Church in Vernon, New Jersey.

"Jack believed in the vision that every person young and not so young should have the opportunity to play tennis as he was able to do as a child and to swim in crystal clear waters in the hot summer days and Crystal Springs Swim and Tennis Club happened. And Jack loved what he saw.

Jack had a vision that families would one day have their homes beside a golf course and that they could drive their golf carts from their homes in the morning, play a round of golf and be back home for lunch. And it happened at Crystal Spring Golf Course. And Jack saw and liked what he saw.

Jack Kurlander did this. But then there was the Playboy Club and Great Gorge Country Club. And then there was The Spa and Black Bear. Jack had a vision. I can design a golf course. If Jack Nicklaus can design golf courses so can Jack Kurlander. And it happened and Jack saw that it was good.

There were those things like Ballyowen and Wild Turkey that Jack envisioned and then happened. And not only did Jack know that they were good, we all knew that they were great.

You all know who you are. Jack had partners along the way. People who helped him bring the vision to fruition. To you today I want you to hear Jack say thank you for helping me make my dreams come true. God Bless You.

Friends, these were some of the accomplishments of Jack Kurlander. There were many, many more. I could go on and on with them. But that's not the kind of Jack Kurlander that I personally want to remember today. I want us to remember Jack Kurlander the man and what it was that made him tick.

Jack was most especially a great husband and a great father. How fortunate it was that the Kurlanders were able to celebrate their 50th anniversary together. And you and I know it wasn't always on the mountaintop with the sun shining that life was lived. Many times it was lived in the valley when the sun was not shining. Jack and Peg believed that no matter what happened they would stand on the mountain again and again and again where the sun shines bright.

Jack Kurlander was an optimist; nothing kept him down. The worst days had great possibilities and he never took time to worry about what was not working, he went on to begin something new.

Last Thursday, I went up to High Point as I do during this time of year to work on a sermon for Sunday. It is a very peaceful place and at the end of my reflections I went up to the Monument at High Point. If you've never been there you should go. You can look out on three states, Pennsylvania, New York and New Jersey and as the sun was setting I looked across the beauty of Pennsylvania and New York and then I crossed to the other side and I looked to Sussex County. As I looked, I could see the remnants of the last bit of melting snow on the clearly visible ski runs in Vernon that was Jack Kurlander's domain – the Sussex County he loved so much. You might say of Jack... Veni, Vidi, Vicum... I came, I saw, I conquered.

Jack was a very caring man. I say that because somebody said that to me yesterday. It didn't matter who Jack Kurlander was sitting down with – either the CEO of a major corporation or the hourly waged individual who was taking out the trash. They were all important to Jack. He made you feel that you were significant and that you meant something to him; that in itself is a great blessing.

Jack Kurlander, as you know, lived with incredible intensity. I truly believe that Jack Kurlander's appointment book was busier than God's. In my 38 years of knowing Jack Kurlander I never saw him walk; the speed was always someplace as if he was doing the 800 yards of the 100 yard dash. I never saw two feet move so fast.

When he wasn't off to a meeting, he was usually heading to the golf course to play against his many golf opponents, where every shot was a challenge, he was not easy and there were few gimmies.

I remember just a few years ago, I realized Jack's intensity and the seriousness with which he took the game when I was playing with him and Pat Schwab who was one of the finest golfers in the State of New Jersey. He was the head teaching pro at the Playboy Club for five years. We were playing at Crystal Springs. Jack once again won and I owed him 6 bucks and in a very kidding way I said to him, "Jack, uh, don't tell me you're going to take 6 bucks from a poor priest." He says, "Father, if you don't have the money, it's okay. Take up a second collection on Sunday and pay me on Monday."

Jack was a generous man. Many of you don't know this. Jack Kurlander helped so many people. He helped young people, he helped old people and he will be rewarded for his generosity.

A few days ago, some mourners at the church described him as a gentleman:

"He was very gentle – he made a difference in my life – he was like a father to me – were it not for him encouraging me, I would never have finished college – you never went by Jack unnoticed even if you were 100 yards away at the end of a parking lot, he waved to you – he was a man who gave me my first job, and he started me on a good road with a great work ethic."

REQUIEM IN PACEM

••••••••••••••••••••••••

Story told by Patrick Coleman, fellow tennis player and friend of Jack

"I entered the men's singles division and after a few matches was paired against Jack Kurlander in the semi-finals which would be played at the Sussex County Tennis Club in Sparta. I lost badly against Jack. The score was 6-1, 6-2. We shook hands, he patted me on the back as I stated that I was really a clay court player. He agreed and told me that I would have won if we had played on clay.

Several months later, I entered a Clay Court Tournament and in the third round, again found myself scheduled to play Jack. It was a tough match with Jack once more emerging as the victor, with a score of 6-4, 6-4. As we met to shake hands, Jack, apparently forgetting what he had said about hard court verses soft court surfaces, patted me on the back and said that I would have won if the game had been played on a hard court. Jack was always a gentleman, and always tried to make people happy."

••••••••••••••••••••••••

JACK, THE BLACK BEAR

Comments made about Jack in April, 2006 – Part of a condolence note received by Jack's family…

"Gentleman, Jack lived a full and vibrant life, showed love to the family and friends, always had a helping hand for others, was a devoted family man and lived his life with great dignity and grace in championship style. And I believe I can see him laughing with God and walking toward his "fairway to heaven". God speed Jack, the Black Bear. You took your best shot, and it was always a beauty. You had a great run, you made your mark and you will be fondly remembered by all who knew you… Your paw prints are all over the hallowed grounds and greens of North Jersey. I know in heaven you will be soaring with the birdies and eagles as you play through to the green, green grass of home."

••••••••••••••••••••••••

John Kurlander's Eulogy

"I'm John Kurlander, Jack's son. I want to share some thoughts with you today about Jack.

Family and friends were the most important things to Jack. I want to let you know that seeing all of you last night and everyone here today makes me feel a great sense of pride and happiness. Your being here demonstrates your affection and respect for Jack. It proves the sharing of his infectious enthusiasm, compassion and indomitable will along with his competitive spirit is an affirmation of how great a man he was.

Jack was a great father to Jamie, Judy and me and a loving and caring husband to Peggy. He was a wonderful and amazing grandfather to our son, Jake, Jamie and Dean's kids Max, Tosh, Tali and Judy and Randolph's son, Evan. Jack and his brother, Bob, along with his wife, Marlene and son Bobby shared a passion for tennis. His brother and sister-in-law from Oregon, Tom and Claire Hekker, shared a passion for having fun with our extended family on a truly grand scale. I'll never forget a summer trip to Oregon in the Winnebago; I was about twelve years old, watching Tom and Jack rope and castrate a young calf. Let me tell you, at twelve years old, that's something that you don't forget.

I spent his last moments on earth with Jack and it's that day that I want to share with you because it is a snapshot of Jack's last day here. When I think back to this past Monday I'm struck by how much of those last hours were representative of Jack's life in general. Preconditions of this trip were not unlike all of his explorations. They blended a love of history, discovery, wonder, conviction, hope and promise. Most importantly, Jack and I were together and I had another opportunity to be with the greatest man I've ever known.

Before I tell you about Jack's last day, I'll try to briefly walk you through my life with my father and our family. Because Jack lived such an incredible and amazing life I'll just be scratching the surface.

Life with Jack was an adventure. My first memories as a child were of the winter – freezing cold weather, deep snow. How many men do you know, who with a fortune consisting of self-confidence, enthusiasm, charisma and a dream would pack up his wife and three children to live in Bennington, Vermont, selling and servicing the world's first automatic ski-waxing machine? Needless to say, when Howard Head invented p-tex which is that plastic material on the base of skis, and put the wooden ski industry out of business with his revolutionary new Head skis, Jack and the rest of the Kurlanders were out of Vermont and back to New Jersey. In this century, with all the buzz words – Jack could not keep track of the buzz words, believe me – I guess he would have been an early adapter. When snowmaking became a viable technology, Jack, after a brief training stint at Craigmeur and Snow Bowl ski areas, then what I am sure was an impassioned sales presentation to Peggy and John and Ann Fitzgerald. He was convinced that New Jersey would be the next ski destination in the US.

But this past Monday promised to be another typical day of adventure and exploration. I know many of you sitting here today know what I am talking about and how exciting it is to be with Jack tracing a dream and a vision and Monday was a snapshot typical of this life. What made Jack's last day important to him was that he was helping plan a new project in a beautiful place; we were meeting with another visionary who had many of the pieces of a new development puzzle in place. And most importantly for Jack, he was with his son, who he loved deeply. Important for me was that I was with my best friend, considering an important development opportunity, but, most important to me was the starting of a cumulative transformation that I was experiencing. Without knowing it at the moment, I realize now that I was beginning to see what Jack has been seeing for years. I was, for the first time, seeing the future potential of a project and I believed that it could happen.

I met Jack at 5:30 Monday morning; he was early, as usual. He had his Dunkin Donuts coffee in hand, there was a half eaten donut lying on the passenger seat – he was surprised at that. He insisted on driving, as usual. Our destination was a small town in northeastern Connecticut known as East Killingly, and we were off to visit an old textile mill built around 1810 and located 25 miles west of Providence, Rhode Island, which happens to be where Jack was born. The project consisted of building housing units in the old mill and building single-family townhomes and condos. To get back to Monday, I wonder now if Jack had thought of his inventor father, a scientist who worked with Thomas Edison and who invented high and low beams for cars and lighthouse optics and flashbulbs for cameras and cinema lighting and gun sites enabling the Japanese to be spotted by Naval gunners when the Japanese would fly in out of the sun and he did that for Bob who was a pilot. That was the reason that a lot of these military inventions were created. Or maybe Jack was preoccupied with thoughts of his father being the Rhode Island state amateur golf champion.

One thing about Jack – he had vision. I had been on many similar trips with him as many of you here today have, I'm sure. I remember walking to the top of Great Gorge with my mother, sisters and the Fitzgeralds when I was six or seven years old and drinking water out of a mountain stream and I'm certain that Peggy, Anna and John Fitzgerald must have asked Jack to tell them again, "Now Jack we're going to build what here? And you say chairlifts are going…where? And we'll have an Austrian ski school?" And sure enough after selling his vision to his family and friends, he launched that vision. What I admired about my father was that he had tremendous strength and he responded to adversity. You couldn't put the man down. He accepted setbacks grudgingly but in the face of all adversity he remained undaunted and certain of his vision that the future would always see improvement and progress and a better life for all people, but most importantly for his friends and family. As proof of Jack's optimism and perseverance, look at what he made happen at Hidden Valley. In the middle of the worst recession this country has known since the Great Depression with interest rates at 18% and cash was king, Jack was again able to pull together family and friends and convince them to build anew. The confidence he was able to generate in people to invest in his vision is astounding. At Crystal Springs I was skeptical of his vision, I didn't see what Jack saw - golf courses and resort living as far as the eye could see. I remember the adventure of exploration and development that began with Black Bear and the Great Gorge Golf Reserve. Jack took Peggy, my wife Ginny and me on a walk through what would become Black Bear, named for a hunting club whose name was posted on the No Trespassing signs that we ignored. At the time, Black Bear was only a collection of dirt paths, thick woods, open fields, wrecked cars, rusty farm equipment and dilapidated buildings. But there was Jack running ahead of us, stopping and waiting for us to catch up… pointing and telling me, "John, we're standing on the tee of number 6, it's a par 5." We would jog on, "And this is the green, and the driving range will be here and the clubhouse here." I can remember thinking – Jack I don't see it, I don't see it. And when you questioned him about the vision, he would just put on a sheepish grin, chuckle, his steely blue eyes would light up and he'd exclaim, "It's going to be great!" And those steely blue eyes could see what no one else could see – he could see the future clear as day. And now, forty-four years after Jack and family moved to the Vernon Valley, I drive along Route 23 in Franklin and see the transformation of an old mining town now bustling with new commercial vigor. Or I drive by Mountain Creek and see the incredible new resort growing out of the ground, and I drive by Crystal Springs and I see a new city growing in front of my eyes, I am surprised and amazed and I now see what Jack saw when he first started chasing his dream, only now it's a reality. So this past Monday when I saw a dilapidated mill on the Connecticut/Rhode Island border just 25 miles away from Jack's birthplace, I started to see it, too. I could see the demolition of parts of the old mill and the building of new housing blended in with this old, failed industry and I felt the conviction that this rundown old property could be something great. I could see it all and most importantly Jack, I, too, believe it can happen. I'm going to miss you but you taught me, and I think you taught many of us sitting here today something important. And that something is that if you can see it, you can make it happen. I think that it's safe to say, on behalf of everyone here, that Jack, we're all starting to see it clearly with you.

Thank you, Jack. We'll meet you on the back nine. No floating mulligans, $5 Nassau, 2-down automatic presses, $3 skins and $1 junk. 'Til then we'll miss you, always love you and thank you for being who you were."

(Tape of John's Eulogy was transcribed by Ginny Cambell)

Memory Lane

Vanity plates for Peg

Kurt Vinson on racing trail

SEASON'S GREETINGS

MEMBER · 80 · 81 · MEMBER · 84 · 85 · hidden valley

Tucker Sno-Cat

Lost Playboy Bunny

Linda, Andy & Peg – thinking of the next prank!

CRYSTAL SPRINGS SWIM & TENNIS CLUB

Lewis & Dollie ready for Hello Dolly Race

Bonnie and Clyde

Nanny Sabina from Germany

Memory Lane

Ground-breaking at HV

Austrian Ski School at GG

Don Decker, Joe Riggs, Larry Marchioni, Don Begraft, Jack

Tennis, swim at Hidden Valley

Landowners courted for Sussex golf courses

Rev. Conway takes ski honors in Great Gorge clergy derby

Poor Light Cause Of Ski Mishaps

BLACK BEAR GOLF & COUNTRY CLUB

Golf Mecca Moving towards Reality
"Pinehurst North" in New Jersey!
by Matthew J. Ward

IT'S COUNTRY PICNIC TIME in SUSSEX COUNTY

Crystal Springs
Hamburg, New Jersey
Box 25 Hamburg, N.J. 07419

For the Discriminating Sportsmen
NORSEMEN "CLUB"

Peg does the finances....

Fun in the money room

NORSEMEN CLUB

Peg assisted by Bud Dunstan — kidding of course

Photo of Gene Mulvihill with Stein Ericksen